Next Generation
Leadership

Next Generation Leadership:
Empowering Youth to Shape the Future of Asia

May 2, 2017
Copyright © 2017 by Center for Asia Leadership Initiatives
Printed in Seoul, Korea

A Publication of the Center for Asia Leadership Initiatives
Acumen Publishing
14 Nancy Lane Waltham MA 02452 USA

Center for Asia Leadership Initiatives
Website: www.asialeadership.org
Facebook: www.facebook.com/asiagroup

Asia Leadership Trek
Website: www.asialeadershiptrek.org
Facebook: www.facebook.com/asialeadershiptrek
Twitter & Weibo: @Asia_Trek

Library of Congress Control Number 2017938471
KDP ISBN: 978-1-5212062-5-6
US $10.99

For inquiries on partnership or sponsorship, or purchase of the publication, please email us at: cali@asialeadership.org

Cover design courtesy of Jin-ok Heo
Typesetting Courtesy of Chun-hee Lee

Next Generation
Leadership

Empowering Youth to Shape the Future of Asia

*22 Youth Leaders Across 9 Countries in
Asia Share Perspectives on Leading Change*

edited by Hungsoo S. Kim

ACUMEN™
PUBLISHING

To all the aspiring leaders of this world

| Table of Contents |

•••

Introduction

Part 1 • Asia Leadership Youth Camp

Part 4 • Trilateral Leadership Summit III

| About the Editor |

•••

Hungsoo S. Kim, a Korean national, is the Co-founder and President of the Center for Asia Leadership Initiatives. Passionate about nurturing and empowering talents in Asia, he has been actively engaging various stakeholders in developing and running over twenty-five programs in more than twenty-two countries in Asia to help emerging leaders explore opportunities to be socially responsible in facing the region's complex challenges. These programs fall under the Center's four main initiatives, namely the Asia Leadership Trek, a public diplomacy arm for scholars at Harvard, Stanford, MIT, and Fletcher; the Asia Leadership Institute, a leadership capacity-building arm; the Acumen Case Center, a research and content development arm; and Acumen Publishing, a publication arm. Hungsoo oversees these initiatives, along with a team of twenty comprising Faculty and Teaching Fellows from Harvard and Stanford University, and administrators at the main office in Boston, U.S., and the Asian regional headquarters in Kuala Lumpur, Malaysia.

As part of his continuous endeavor toward grooming leaders of tomorrow, Hungsoo recently joined the Asia Future Institute, a Seoul-based policy and leadership think tank, as Executive Director to instill in Korean and Northeast Asian talents the drive and passion to create positive social change through effective leadership. He prides himself on accelerating efforts to reach out to all forty-eight countries in Asia by 2022. Hungsoo's areas of research and training, among others, include 'Negotiation and Mediation,' 'Adaptive Leadership,' 'Persuasion and Influence,' and 'Creative Confidence.' To date, some twenty-five thousand burgeoning and established leaders from the government, non-profits, and corporate world in Asia have benefited from these programs.

Prior to establishing the Center, Hungsoo worked for twelve years in varying sectors from strategy consulting and social entrepreneurship to international development, politics, and government. He has also served as a policy aide in the United Nations in New York representing Korea, and as a project analyst at UNESCO in Paris. He currently sits on the board of two non-profit organizations, and has served as a visiting scholar at the Asia Center at Harvard University and at the Kellogg School of Management in Northwestern University. Hungsoo holds a Masters of Public Administration from the Harvard Kennedy School of Government; Masters in International Cooperation from the Graduate School of International Studies, Seoul National University; and completed his undergraduate studies with two majors in U.S. and International Law, and International Politics with a minor in Economics from Handong University.

Previously, Hungsoo was the editor of four books, namely Rethinking Asia Vol. 1: Education and Innovation, *Rethinking Asia Vol. 2: Entrepreneurship and Economic Development, Finding the Leaders in Us: New Goals for the Future, and Redefining Success: Learning to Lead for Change. He is the editor of three upcoming books scheduled for release in May entitled, Rethinking Asia Vol. 3: Social and Political Change, Next Generation Leadership: Empower Youth to Shape the Future of Asia, and Leaders in Development: Enhancing Your Leadership Effectiveness in a Changing World.*

| About the Contributors |

•••

Hungsoo S. Kim is the Co-founder and President of the Center for Asia Leadership Initiatives. Passionate about nurturing and empowering talents in Asia, he has developed and organized over twenty-five programs in more than twenty-two countries in the region to help budding leaders enhance their leadership competencies to navigate challenges in the 21st century. Hungsoo aims to engage with youth in all forty-eight countries in Asia by 2022 and inspire them to enact change in the world.

Janice Tan Sue Wei was born on July 8, 2001 in Petaling Jaya, Malaysia. She plays the piano and violin, and enjoys art and traveling. Janice is in Year 11 at Sri KDU International School, Malaysia and aspires to become a doctor one day.

Michelle S Lee is an avid tennis player and is passionate about contributing positively to the local community. She was the Executive Director for the 24-Hour Race KL 2016 and is the Secretary General for Malaysia National Model UN 2017. She is currently an undergraduate degree candidate at Minerva Schools at KGI, United States.

Bryan Chay is a fifteen-year-old Singaporean living in Malaysia. He loves sports and volunteering at charities involving children. Bryan is currently studying in Year 11 at the Alice Smith School, Malaysia.

Jonson Tham is a hardworking Grade 10 student at Sunway International School, Malaysia who does his best to achieve his hopes and dreams. He considers his contribution to this book as a stepping stone toward future accomplishments.

Ben Ang Zi Qi is an adventurous person who likes exploring new ideas. He is a wannabe writer and enjoys sharing his experiences with others. Ben is currently studying A–Levels at Sunway College, Malaysia and will be sitting for his A2 Examinations this May.

Kamaleshwaran Ganeson is a nineteen-year-old Psychology student at Sunway University, Malaysia. A cat lover, Kamaleshwaran enjoys playing video games in his free time and engaging in thought-provoking conversations with people from all walks of life.

Ong Qian Chern loves nature as much as he loves watching basketball games. A simple stroll in the park lets him unwind and relax. Currently pursuing an IT degree in computer networking and security at Sunway University, Malaysia, Qian Chern dreams of becoming a network specialist and connecting people from around the world via the internet.

Loh Lynn Way is currently pursuing the Canadian International Matriculation Program (CIMP) at Sunway College, Malaysia. She is a member of the CIMP Student Council and a sub-editor for TheLifeAgent.co. Lynn Way has always played an active role in school and was the Vice President of the Leo Club at her secondary school, SMK Subang Utama, Malaysia.

Mengheng Lim works as a civil engineer in Phnom Penh, Cambodia. With a deep passion for social entrepreneurship, he has been engaged in research projects that aim to improve the state of the construction industry as well as traffic congestion in Cambodia.

Maika Tsuchiya was born in Japan and has been raised by her grandmother since she was four years old. While her hobbies include watching musicals and singing, her dream is to become a biologist and learn about regenerative medicine to develop new treatment methods for diseases believed to be incurable.

Amirhossein Rahbari is a science student at Sunway College, Malaysia. His passion for helping people is what keeps him motivated, in hopes that one day he could fulfil his dream and follow his passion to become a surgeon to save lives.

Aleksandra Kan is a twenty-two-year-old student at the Gubkin Russian State University of Oil and Gas in Tashkent. She is studying at the Faculty of Operation and Maintenance of Gas Production Facilities, Gas Condensate and Underground Storage Facilities. Aleksandra is passionate about foreign languages and is currently learning English and Korean. A firm believer in the importance of human connections, Aleksandra enjoys discovering different cultures and hopes to exchange knowledge, skills and experience with people from all over the world.

Anastasiia Iun was born in Osh, Fergana Valley, the biggest city in southern Kyrgyzstan. She is a behavior analyst at the Bishkek Center for Autism and Applied Behavior Analysis. Anastasiia attributes her passion to work with autistic children to her strong family values that emphasize education, modesty, healthy relationships with people and personal contribution to society. Her favorite quote is "And whoever saves a life, it is considered as if he saved an entire world" by Talmud, and hopes to contribute to the improvement of people's psychological well-being.

Anjela Kamalova was born in 1995 in the Tashkent region, Uzbekistan. She is a fourth-year student at the Tashkent State Institute of Oriental Studies, Uzbekistan and specializes in Japanese language and culture. Anjela, a third-generation Korean, is also learning the Korean language to get in touch with her roots.

Evgeniy Kim is a twenty-two-year-old student who is pursuing a Bachelor's Degree in Business Administration at the Westminster International University in Tashkent, Uzbekistan. Her hobbies include playing the guitar and snowboarding. Evgeniy enjoys exploring new things and is also learning Korean at the Center of Culture and Education of the Republic of Korea in Tashkent.

Zarina Shemdanova was born on May 11, 1995 in Tashkent, Uzbekistan. She is currently studying Korean language and literature at Tashkent State Pedagogical University Named After Nizami, Uzbekistan. In her pastime, she enjoys reading, watching movies and listening to music.

Megumi Konishi is a high school student currently studying in Japan. She grew up in London and spent much of her childhood traveling, which sparked her interest in international relations and global issues. In the future, she would like to take this further and study human rights issues around the world.

Annie Dawon Lee is a Senior at Phillips Academy in Andover, Massachusetts, United States. Born in Seoul, Korea, Annie lived in Toronto, Canada for six years prior to attending boarding school near Boston, Massachusetts, United States. She is the News Editor of her school's weekly paper and a cellist in the school orchestra.

Shiina Yuri was born in Kyoto, Japan in 1998. The high school student is interested in law and politics, and hopes to gain as much knowledge and skills as possible to realize her dream of becoming her country's future leader. Shiina's hobbies include jogging with friends and playing the piano.

Jiho Hwang loves writing about international issues and is currently working as a journalist with the Korea Youth Press Corps. Her interests include writing, reading and swimming. She believes in trying new things and looks forward to embracing opportunities to broaden her horizon. The high school student hopes to further her studies overseas to gain invaluable knowledge and experience.

Alex Wookyung Lee has a keen interest in Biology and Philosophy, and aims to pursue both areas of study when she attends university. With an ambition to become a scientist and philosopher, Alex wishes to examine human science, neuroscience, genetics and evolutionism from a philosophical perspective.

Hinako Telengut was born in Sapporo, Hokkaido, Japan. The seventeen-year-old is a second-grade student at Ritsumeikan Keisho High School. Hinako is interested to study Mathematics, Physics and International Relations when she enters university.

Introduction

| Introduction |

The Power of Youth –
Building a Better Tomorrow

Hungsoo S. Kim

● ●●

Throughout my career, I have been privileged to work with a diverse group of people across different fields. I find it especially rewarding to work with youth, engaging with the young generation and finding out what makes them tick. At the Center for Asia Leadership Initiatives (CALI), we are committed to focusing on youth development and exploring their needs, experiences, and potential contributions to society. I was excited and pleased to welcome a wonderful group of energetic and passionate youth to our four Asia Leadership Youth and Scholars (ALYS) programs in 2016: the Asia Leadership Youth (ALY) Camp in Malaysia; the Global Leadership Trek (GLT) in the U.S.; the Central Asia Youth Leadership Camp (CALC), co-organized by CALI and the Korea Development Bank (KDB) Foundation in Pohang, Korea; and the Trilateral Leadership Summit III (TLS) in Incheon, Korea.

I spent a large part of my youth in the Philippines because of my parents' decision to leave Korea and work in the humanitarian sector, helping to develop Southeast Asian countries. As a child of parents who devoted their lives to the betterment of disadvantaged communities, I learned at an early age about the hardships experienced by the less fortunate. At times we lived the way they did, in humble conditions, lacking even the smallest luxuries, such as running water and electricity. This environment allowed me to look at life from a different point of view, and that in turn led me to a journey of self-discovery.

Many years ago, the Philippines was at its peak economically, while Korea was one of the poorest countries in the world. I remember how Korea looked up to the Philippines, viewing it as a role model for economic success. Today offers a different story: Korea, once an economic wasteland, has admirably transformed itself into a developed nation, becoming one of the world's great success stories. As for the Philippines—sadly, the one-time industrial powerhouse of Asia has experienced crippling economic setbacks, due to mismanagement by its leadership. Observing these changes of fortune made me realize the importance of education and effective leadership in spurring a nation's development and prosperity. I strongly believe that everyone, and especially youth, should have equal access to a good education and opportunities for growth, regardless of their financial backgrounds. Only the vibrancy and enthusiasm of the young generation can bring about change and make tomorrow better than today. This belief, which my co-founders at CALI share, led us to the development of the ALYS program.

The ALYS program is not a typical youth program, designed to keep young people occupied during the holidays. Instead, it comprises residential programs organized all over the world, which enable youth to discover themselves and learn how to be effective future leaders. Its programs expose participants to current issues and today's leadership challenges through "deep-dive" plenary sessions, interactive workshops, special talks, networking opportunities, and evening activities, all encouraging greater interaction among the youth. These activities enable youth to develop crucial leadership skills and practices, including negotiating, managing thought processes, asking good questions, public speaking, developing cultural intelligence, cultivating innovative and creative capacities, and building personal branding. The ALYS programs also provide individual and small group career coaching and professional development seminars, which help the students write and deliver good speeches, create resumes, manage stress, succeed in interviews, manage career derailers, develop financial literacy, discover entrepreneurship essentials, build social media brands, give elevator pitches, make great first impressions, network, and—perhaps most importantly—navigate the application process for overseas universities. Fostering an environment that encourages every participant to take part in the activities, the ALYS allows students to nurture essential relationships with others and acquire essential skills that will kickstart their careers in the near future.

One unique aspect of each ALYS program is the presence of knowledgeable and devoted Teaching Fellows, primarily from Harvard University and Stanford University, who actively embrace their roles as mentors and coaches for the participants. Mentors are crucial figures not only because they teach important lessons but also because they assure young people that capable adults care about their well-being and wish them nothing but the best. Often they help the young deal with everyday challenges and guide them in identifying their strengths, so that they can unlock their full potential. Throughout my life, I have been fortunate enough to benefit from several mentors and coaches who helped me grow and get through tough times. These relationships can have a powerful and positive impact on young people in their personal, academic, and professional lives. In the ALYS, we provide mentors with expertise in a wide range of fields. I myself have worked in management consulting, diplomacy, politics, the army, social entrepreneurship, and non-profit management. All the Teaching Fellows do their best to share their knowledge and expertise with the participants, and the participants go home not only with new lifelong friends from many different cultures but also with a deep sense of connection with the Teaching Fellows.

The Four Programs of the ALYS

In the ALY Camp held in Kuala Lumpur, high school students get the chance to learn how to prepare for the leadership challenges that they will face in their personal, professional, and social lives, as well as how to translate their values into meaningful and material action. This is supported by workshops and activities such as 'building character and enhancing collaboration capacity,' 'practice of negotiation,' 'building meta-thinking skills,' 'building 21st century core competencies,' 'defining a context for success,' 'building techniques for confident self-promotion,' 'how to make effective decisions,' and 'building and using networks as a source of intelligence and influence.'

The GLT, an opportunity to learn through experience, was inspired by the original Asia Leadership Trek (ALT), CALI's flagship initiative that began in 2012. Offering opportunities for socioeconomic, political, and cultural study, the GLT provides a unique, first-hand learning experience through a tour of three U.S. cities—New York, Washington, D.C., and Boston. It caters exclusively to the needs of young emerging leaders in Asia, and it consists of two central elements: (1) organized meetings with U.S. thought leaders and decision makers from various industries and areas of expertise, from whom participants can learn what makes the U.S. a leading nation in the world in the fields of education, innovation, social leadership, and entrepreneurship; (2) a three-day camp in which the participants develop leadership skills and seek the improvement of self, others, and the community. Participants can discuss their own areas of interest and are given background information and tools with which to enact positive change in those areas.

The CALC is a six-week program for Korean youth in Central Asia. Teaching Fellows from Harvard offer mentorship, inspirational stories, discussions on best practices, and capacity-building workshops about positive change, leadership, and social-profit initiatives, namely entrepreneurship, innovation in education, and social responsibility. The CALC program trains participants in crucial leadership principles that will enable them to navigate the ever-changing world once they embark on their careers.

The TLS is an international program designed to help Chinese, Japanese, and Korean high school students tackle challenges faced by the Northeast Asian region. The program employs elements from the Harvard Kennedy School's "U.S. Congress and Law Making" and "Adaptive Leadership" courses, as well as Stanford Design School's theories of design thinking and innovation. In addition to its interactive workshops, professional development sessions, and career mentoring, the TLS gives students the opportunity to take part in a trilateral summit simulation, promoting inter-country dialogue, networking, increased awareness, and collaborative skill development.

As the world becomes more globalized, it is increasingly vital for students to expand their horizons and open their minds. Unfortunately, memorization is the default way of learning in the Asian education system. Our programs, by contrast, allow students to actively engage in high-level learning processes that strengthen critical thinking and creative problem solving skills through a framework of knowing, doing, and being. Their dramatic results can be seen in the overwhelmingly positive responses from participants in such diverse countries like Bangladesh, Iran, Cambodia, Malaysia, Japan, Korea, China, Kyrgyzstan, Uzbekistan, Kazakhstan, and the U.S.

In these personal essays, I hope you will enjoy the authors' personal reflections and come away with key insights from their experiences. The book as a whole reflects the authors' commitment to making a difference in the world; the essays describe their observations of other cultures and emphasize the relevance of cross-cultural competencies in the globalized world. Overall, the book depicts a multi-faceted, collaborative journey of self-discovery, as the students learn about 21st century leadership skills and the importance of embracing change.

Moving forward, we at CALI aim to set the trend in life-changing learning experiences for youth around the world, as they carve their paths into the future. Today, students must start planning their professional development at a young age and fill their holidays with educational programs that will help prepare them for later lives. Students are the leaders of today and tomorrow, and they have a responsibility to bring about positive social change. With this in mind, CALI is dedicated to introducing world-leading best practices to Asia, in adaptive leadership, innovative education, and value creating entrepreneurship, with the aim of shaping an equitable and sustainable future for all. We envision an Asia filled with strong and enthusiastic youth who together push for advocacy, social entrepreneurship, and activism throughout the region.

Our programs have the ability to empower young people by providing them with the resources, skill sets, knowledge, networking contacts, and opportunities they need to succeed. We help them to influence others not only in their communities but across the globe. As we pass the baton to the young generation, it is my great hope that today's youth will raise awareness and educate people about the pressing issues of our time. It takes courage to undertake such colossal responsibility, but with the necessary tools and expertise, our youth have the power to create the change we hope to see in the world.

So go ahead and take up the challenge. Let your actions speak louder than your words. The future is yours for the taking!

Part 1

:

Asia Leadership
Youth Camp

| Chapter 1 |

Time to Soar Like the Phoenix

Janice Tan Sue Wei

● ● ●

In Greek mythology, a phoenix is a long-lived bird that is cyclically reborn. Associated with the sun, a phoenix obtains new life by arising from the ashes of its previous life. Like the phoenix, I desired to become a different person and have a new beginning. The Asia Leadership Youth (ALY) Camp represents the stage of rebirth, while the ashes are my old self.

Before this life-changing experience, I was an insecure naïve girl. I was born into a normal family, just like most of you who are reading this. Living in a pressure-filled world took its toll on me. Social pressure is real, and it's hovering around us right now. You become a victim when you forget your true qualities and what you stand for. You succumb to it when you change yourself in order to be accepted by society. I always wear a mask to deceive others, pretending that I am strong and confident. But deep down, until recently, there was a timid, different girl who doubted her purpose of existence and constantly questioned her role in life. Ever since I was young, I have been socially awkward, which resulted in my becoming an outcast in school. It's always a struggle trying to fit in and to be accepted as an equal. I would hide at the back of the class, pilling stacks of books in front of me to shield myself from the rest of the world.

In high school, there always seems to be a stereotypically popular group of girls who saunter down the school hallways. Like other 'popular' groups, they fit the image of being vain, conceited, judgmental, dramatic and abnormally thin. I have come to the realization, by judging others by their physical appearance and sometimes their personality, people can be hurtful and destructive. In one of William Shakespeare's tragedies, *Macbeth*, the protagonist is consumed by his ambition to be the King of Scotland. Macbeth feels the need to prove his manhood and his love for his wife, Lady Macbeth, so strongly that he kills King Duncan in order to take the Scottish throne for himself. In the end, he regrets his actions and comes to believe that his soul can never be cleansed from the sin. One might argue that insecurity led to the downfall of Macbeth. The play shows that insecurity is a silent killer and that anyone could fall prey to it.

In my early teenage years, I struggled with the ideal of being perfect. I tried to fit the social standards of being popular. I once had a best friend: beautiful, smart, kind and sporty, she seemed perfect in everyone's eyes. I was the total opposite, plain and boring. But I felt the need to be as pretty and as smart as she was in order to fit in. She was my best friend yet my greatest enemy, for she made me hate myself even more. People liked to compare me to her, and she was always the most favored one. My insecurities led me to think that she would one day come to her senses and feel that I was not good enough to be her friend. True enough, she did eventually dump me, and I lost my best and only friend. I punished myself by becoming anorexic, assuming that it was my fault that she left me. Other students at the school bullied me, and I felt isolated. I dreaded going to school, which for me was filled with cruel and judgmental people. During lunch breaks, I would lock myself in the toilet, silently weeping. My once cheerful and free-spirited self was gone. I lost a piece of my soul and had no purpose in life; I had forgotten my core values.

My life improved dramatically when I attended the ALY Camp. In the beginning, I was scared that I would be treated as unfairly and indifferently as I was in school. I worried about being an outcast at the ALY Camp—not to mention that I would be living in a foreign environment for a week and was expected to share with my roommates. When I arrived my heart was beating fast and I could feel butterflies in my stomach. But as the saying goes, 'After every storm, there is a rainbow.' Unexpectedly, I made friends and managed to be accepted. At first it was a challenge for me to socialize with others. I was awkward and constantly fidgeted with my fingers when I was forced to make conversation. I envied those who were sociable and could easily get along with everyone. Most of the time, I remained quiet and spoke only when I was spoken to. During my first discussion in Ms. Lisa Lee's class on survival in the desert, I was the quietest one and kept my thoughts and opinions to myself. I was nervous and afraid of being wrong and judged by the other delegates. Although my peers encouraged me to contribute, I still kept to myself. But, strangely enough, the results showed that I work better in a group compared to individually. This made me realize that I actually had something to offer that could really benefit the group.

As we progressed, I managed to hit it off with my two roommates. We were very different in personality, yet similar in some ways too. Both of my roommates were very sociable and managed to make me feel comfortable. For the first time in a long while, I felt that I was being treated as an equal. It was a new experience. I wasn't seen as the girl I used to be. I was seen as a new person. As a result, I felt a slight boost of confidence. The week unfolded slowly, with heaps of homework and endless class discussions. Soon I even started to get along with people from different backgrounds and age groups. The interaction during class discussions really broke the ice. We talked, shared our thoughts and laughed at each other's jokes. I began to warm up to other people and was able to hold long conversations. Moreover, I learned interesting facts from my fellow delegates. They all came from different backgrounds and were there for many different reasons. It was truly a breath of fresh air. The ALY Camp provided a completely new experience for me. It enabled me to become better and more sure of myself. For instance, I recently went to a college interview, feeling more confident than ever before. The ALY Camp pushed me to my limits and also taught me useful skills, such as speechwriting and public speaking. I came home with a brand new outlook on life, and I know the skills and knowledge that I gained at the ALY Camp will help me in the long run.

Mr. Randy Tarnowski's workshop provided me with refreshing insights into the key elements of leadership communication. Aristotle's theory of Logos, Ethos and Pathos really resonated with me. To be honest, initially I had doubts about the lessons at the ALY Camp, Mr. Tarnowski quickly washed them away. He was an inspiring Teaching Fellow, and I truly enjoyed his lessons. I could sense that he applied the Aristotle theory in his lessons by finding common ground with the delegates. I also discovered that all great speeches made by pre-eminent leaders around the world fit the framework of Logos, Ethos and Pathos. Logos means content and logic, Ethos means character, credibility and characteristics, and Pathos means emotional connection and adhesion. For example, the Winston Churchill speech that we read had trust, character and emotion. The speech we read by Donovan Livingston fascinated me because it was a poem that made me feel the emotion between the lines. It was passionate and, most importantly, original. The speech we read by President Obama was uplifting and motivating. In his speech, he managed to connect with the audience and respond to the everyday concerns of the people, which humanized him for his listeners. Repetition was used to show contrast and importance, while inclusive words were incorporated to show why our community is called upon to act.

In the 'Entrepreneurship Leadership' workshop, I became more aware of the refugee issue in Malaysia. I learned that refugees are different from illegal immigrants, and yet they are not recognized as citizens and are treated poorly, with no access to public education or jobs. We were given the opportunity to speak to representatives of the United Nations High Commission for Refugees (UNHCR) as well as real-life refugees. The refugees are still not treated as equals, despite having refugee identification cards. They are just like all of us, but people's negative attitude toward them has affected their sense of identity and belonging, as well as their sense of a purpose in life. They are concerned about their uncertain future. The government turns a blind eye to them by not providing them with suitable jobs; sometimes it even sends the police to arrest them. One refugee shared a story of how his refugee identification card, along with other valuables, were taken away from him by the police. There were even cases when the authorities took advantage of the refugees' vulnerability. This upset me, and I felt empathetic toward the refugees because they were not treated fairly. The lesson struck me hard by exposing me to current world issues. The refugees are stuck, since they do not want to seek help from society and become dependent. All they want is get a job, work hard, provide for their family and have a better life. It made me realize how blessed I am to be born into a loving family and to have every opportunity to do what the refugees are yearning for.

Thinking about the refugees' daily struggles impacted me in a big way, especially during the class discussion in which we had to try to solve the refugee issue. My group and I came up with a solution to help refugee children. Most of the volunteer teachers do not have enough training to teach the refugees effectively. Statistics even show that many people want to educate refugees but are unable to do so due to their lack of expertise. Our plan was to train volunteer teachers for a span of one to two years. Given the advent of social media, we decided that promoting the cause via Facebook Ads would be the best way forward. We hoped that in this way refugee children would gain access to better education, particularly English and Mathematics. With these basic skills, the refugee children would have a better chance at gaining independence and a stable job in the future, thus ensuring a better life for themselves and their family. Even though this might not be the best solution to the refugee crisis, I believe that small acts, when multiplied by millions of people, can transform the world.

Mr. John Lim's '21st Century Lessons' were enjoyable, fun and energetic. Even though it was the last lesson of each day, his sessions always held my full attention and restored my energy. One of my favorite activities was the marshmallow challenge. It may sound like a game, but it taught me the importance of teamwork and communication. I also discovered five new skills for communicating. First, I learned to manage emotion by having a moral compass. Second, I learned that listening and getting the message across are important in avoiding a natural egocentric bias. Third and fourth, I learned not to behave defensively and to build trust. Trust is crucial even in a short activity. We need to trust each other so that the activity can benefit everyone. I used to think trust was a road to disappointment. Mr. Lim, however, made me see it as a completely different thing. We are in charge of our destiny, and we should take leaps of faith because life is full of surprises and risks. It's up to us to make these decisions. Lastly, I learned the importance of discovering what motivates others, for leaders must be able to inspire their people. Even though these skills are most appropriate for the business world, I know I can apply them when I'm communicating with others in my daily life.

Mr. Lim also taught us how to write a good resume. 'The devil is in the details,' he told us. It is important to pay attention to the small things, including font size and alignment, as this reflects what kind of person you are. Mr. Lim told us that our world is very competitive and always changing. Hence, we need to start noticing the little things to stay ahead of the competition.

Goals are what you need to achieve purpose. My role models are Nelson Mandela and J.K. Rowling. Nelson Mandela was courageous and fought for what he believed in, and, because of his efforts, South Africa is no longer torn apart by apartheid. Persistence also paid off for J.K. Rowling. She was rejected by publishers many times, but that did not deter her; she kept going and never gave up. Today, she is one of the most renowned authors in the world. The values of both Mandela and Rowling are inspiring. Before the ALY Camp, I didn't know my purpose, dreams, goals and values. But people like Nelson Mandela and J.K. Rowling have shown me that anyone can be successful as long as they put their mind and heart to it.

For me, the defining moment of the ALY Camp was the speech competition. Due to my lack of confidence, public speaking has always scared me. Ever since I can remember, I have had terrible stage fright. My fingers tremble, and my mind goes completely blank. When I first heard about the speech competition, I felt petrified. Even when I practiced in front of my roommates, my whole body was shaking and I stuttered a lot. Fortunately, they were very supportive and encouraging. Moreover, they gave me helpful feedback and useful tips. On the day of the competition itself, I mustered all the courage in me and gave it my all. My peers congratulated me and gave me constructive criticism. Even though I didn't make it to the final round, I was still proud of my achievement. The feeling after I had finished was amazing, indescribable. I felt like a completely different person after that four-minute speech. Besides that, it was heartening to hear other people's speeches, especially the ones chosen for the top three. These speeches were moving and relatable to all of us, clearly showing elements of Ethos, Pathos and Logos. I was especially drawn to the speech made by my roommate, Marianne Lim, about self-acceptance. Even though her speech didn't make it to the final round, it was my favorite. Her speech taught me to walk away from my insecurities and become a new person.

Another major defining moment was when I had to perform random acts of kindness. My group and I decided to give out free compliments and flyers to random strangers at the Sunway Pyramid Shopping Mall. It was hard at first because we encountered lots of rejections and harsh remarks. I stumbled over my words when I approached someone. However, my fellow delegates were very supportive, and, with time, I got the hang of it. I even got used to the rejections and gained confidence along the way.

Recently, I saw an iconic photo taken by Kevin Carter in March of 1993. It is a heartbreaking photo of an emaciated Sudanese toddler with a vulture nearby, watching the girl with a keen eye, waiting for her to die. In that photo, the beast has triumphed over man. Carter eventually won the Pulitzer Prize for the image. However, he had not helped the toddler and was bombarded with questions about her. Consumed with guilt, he committed suicide a year later. The photo is known as a 'metaphor for Africa's despair' and motivated me to try to fight cruelty and to ensure that more children obtain access to basic needs. Stuart Avery Gold, in his book *Ping!* states, "Unless you dream of it, the dream will never begin and come to life." My dream is to change the world by ending poverty. My goal is to reduce food waste and hunger, especially among children, who are victims of the greedy and uncaring world.

Nowadays, newspapers are filled with reports of killings and multiple attacks. The world is seen as a dangerous and fearful place. And, according to the United Nations, approximately twenty-one thousand people die every day due to poverty. That is one every four seconds, and sadly children are the ones most affected by these tragedies. This is mainly because of the world's economic systems, which do not promote inclusive growth and as a result allow the rich to get richer and the poor to get poorer. Working with the refugees made me see that we are all the same. Even though we come from different environments, we still have a lot in common. I found it fun and exciting working with new people. The refugees were each unique; they surpassed my expectations, and I felt ashamed for thinking lowly of them. They have dreams to fulfil and much to contribute to our society. I'm glad that the ALY Camp gave me the opportunity to meet them.

Ephesians 2:10 says, 'We are God's workmanship, created in Christ Jesus to do good works, which God prepared in advance for us to do.' This is God's answer to me about finding my purpose. I want to put a stop to poverty. I was put into this world at this time in order to change it and to make it a better place for everyone. With useful tools like S.W.O.T. (Strengths, Weaknesses, Opportunities, Threats), I was able to utilize my strengths to minimize my threats and weaknesses. With my values and strengths, I discovered new opportunities. For example, I decided to start doing simple things like donating and volunteering on missionary trips. Furthermore, I rediscovered myself by opening up and socializing with more people. The poet William Ernest Henley once wrote, 'I am the master of my fate, I am the captain of my soul.' At the ALY Camp, I stepped out of my comfort zone and realized that I can do things beyond my wildest imagination.

Throughout my teenage years, I was weak, insecure, timid and scared. Now, I am not, and I owe it all to the ALY Camp. God has a bigger plan for me than I have for myself. From this day onwards, I am a risen phoenix. I am determined to become a new and improved person so that I can change the world. I want to be remembered as someone who made a difference, and the ALY Camp has put me on that path. It taught me that we are future leaders and that we can create change. We need to stay true to our core values and not succumb to social pressure. We are the leaders of ourselves.

Challenge yourself. Use that as fuel to motivate you to reach your desired goals. Fear is our energy. Each time we overcome our fear or overcome a struggle, we become stronger.

| Chapter 2 |

Connecting to the World Around You

Michelle S Lee

● ● ●

Ever since I was a child, I've loved and obsessed over all different forms of media: books, movies, music, games. I read, watched and listened to as many as I could and hoarded their physical forms whenever possible. I loved media for the stories they told. Even with the more abstract forms of media, like music and visual art, I coveted those that held more narrative structures, those that somehow told a story. When I recall the memories that have stuck with me since I was young, they're often connected to some form of media: nights at the movies with my parents, dancing to my favorite band at camp or playing games at the neighbors'. Media has always been an incredibly important form of expression for me.

As a result, I have been known as reclusive, preferring the encapsulating company of stories to that of other people. To me, a night curled up in bed with a book, curtains drawn, music blasting, obligations non-existent and reality dulled, is much more attractive than a night out at a dinner party, where life is gridlocked by social rules and friendly obligations. Perhaps I also have competitive tendencies and leaned toward comparison—bad habits I am aware of but still cannot fully break.

I'm not a shy or quiet person either. If you were to ask everybody I've met to make a list of adjectives that would sum up my personality, most people (including me) would list 'loud,' and many would include 'playful' and 'stubborn.' So, I'm not by nature a socially awkward person—though I can be sometimes—it's just that I don't regularly enjoy human company, at least in comparison to a new book or a must-watch movie.

When I first arrived for the ALY Camp, I was greeted by the Student Leaders: helpful, friendly and excited individuals all wanting to do whatever they could to make me feel as comfortable as possible. I was standing there with a suitcase larger than my overall frame, a backpack and seven clothes-hangers' worth of formal clothing. The Student Leaders hurried over to placate my parents' worries, relieve me of my luggage and escort me to the registration counter. I viewed their behavior as the ideal, correct one that I should emulate throughout my time at the ALY Camp, and the weight of that necessity frightened me. I wanted to be the bright, charming individual whose company was enjoyed by those around me, and that very desire created my abhorrence for situations that would allow that to happen.

On our first day, in the 'Personal Branding' plenary session led by Mr. Hungsoo S. Kim, we heard stories of successful individuals: the hardships they came across as well as their successes and motivations. Examples included Picasso and his unsold paintings, which numbered over nine hundred; Abraham Lincoln, who endured the tragic deaths of his loved ones; and Walt Disney, who couldn't find employment because of being 'uncreative.' Then Mr. Kim talked about his own stories and his background of poverty, how he strived to be rich one day—yet, when he finally had the cash, he gave it all away to the poor. These stories, especially Mr. Kim's, really touched the class and made us question how much we took for granted and how much our world needed people to strive for the betterment of our community and society.

Then we had to hold interview sessions with people we'd never talked to before. I met a person with a difficult childhood and a family that disapproved of his identity, except for his mentor, his mother. His obvious respect and affection for her, coupled with his difficult family background, made me re-evaluate my appreciation for my own family. We talked about our approaches to life and our views of success, what we thought of the public education system in Malaysia and societal stereotypes, and our opinions of things that I didn't think most people around me were comfortable discussing. For the first time in a long time, I felt connected to someone else.

Mr. Kim also taught us how to work on our personal branding, requiring us to identify our core motivations and ideals, then personify them through a logo that we had to come up with. We stayed up until the small hours of the morning, discussing and planning these logos, from their shapes to their colors to their symbolism. We were so focused on representing ourselves that in our Milo-fueled daze, we didn't even realize that we had exchanged our most private stories. In between impromptu martial arts classes, homegrown rap remixes and honest down-to-business hard work, we'd openly shared and connected our personalities and drive.

Mr. Kim also taught the workshop 'Negotiation Leadership.' He described two different types of negotiation: Distributive and Cumulative. Distributive Negotiation is about claiming value from the other party, whereas Cumulative Negotiation is about increasing value for everybody involved. We were given various negotiation exercises that encapsulated these theories, requiring us to negotiate with each other after receiving separate briefs. The takeaway insight we gained—after creating mostly subpar deals for all parties involved—was the importance of creating value through information exchange: finding each other's Best Alternative to a Negotiated Agreement (BATNA) and expanding the Zone of Possible Agreement (ZOPA) accordingly. I learned many applicable skills, particularly in negotiations with event sponsors, but what stuck with me the most was Mr. Kim's emphasis on the latter type of negotiation. In Cumulative Negotiation, he emphasized the importance of exchanging information, to find out what each party valued most and what each party had to offer in order to create the best deal for everybody involved. For example, a part-time employee may prioritize experiences and flexible working hours, whereas an employer may prioritize salary and long-term commitment—hence an agreement can be negotiated to give each party the best of their priorities, at the expense of their non-priorities. The process necessitates viewing the other party as a partner, rather than an adversary.

When we think of culture, we often think of clothes, food, buildings, etc.—things that undeniably symbolize culture but do not fully explain it. If you saw only the traditional clothes and food, would you know what that culture was all about? In 'Cross-Cultural Competencies', taught by Teaching Fellow, Mr. Randy Tarnowski, we learned his definition of culture: 'values and beliefs held by a group of people.' We discussed, analyzed, and compared world cultures, organizational cultures and personal cultures, studying how they affected and enhanced each other. To a background of smooth jazz and mutual respect, we discussed and debated the nuances of Malaysian culture(s); we discussed the different subcultures within Malaysia, the values that each upheld (or denounced), and how they influenced each other. We talked about all of this under Mr. Tarnowski's prompting guidance and on top of Hofstede's Cultural Dimensions theory, which he taught us. The conversation quickly got more intense than most of us were prepared for; as Mr. Tarnowski put it, 'I wanted to dip my feet in, but now I'm drowning.' We soon got past the surface image of the Malaysia we wanted to portray and into the deeply flawed systems that ran everything below it. Classes with Mr. Tarnowski served as igniting sparks for many of our discussions outside class on culture, globalization and our community.

Meanwhile, Teaching Fellow, Ms. Lisa Lee taught us about finding a solution for the refugee crisis in Malaysia. Ms. Lee had crafted a Design Thinking project in her time at the Harvard Graduate School of Education, and this was the model that we used in creating our project. Over literal mounds of Post-It notes, we discussed the issue we most wanted to tackle, talked to stakeholders, did our own research, created an action plan and pitched our final product to stakeholders and other students. We learned a lot about the issue and, subtly, about each other. Working together on the issue wasn't always easy, and we didn't always begin on the same page—it was obvious that some team members cared more about the issue than others. But discussions with stakeholders and the stories of their experiences warmed even the coldest and indifferent hearts. Moreover, our discussions revealed our strengths and weaknesses, leading us to capitalize on our strengths and mitigate each other's weaknesses. Communication, we learned early on, was necessary for smoothing out kinks in our team and, by conjunction, our project.

Beyond internal communication, our discussions with the stake-holders revealed the greatest problem in all of our projects: sympathy over empathy. All of us wanted to provide food, aid and education to the refugees. We wanted to help the lost, straggled and helpless people who washed up on our shores, but we forgot that most of them had lives before they became refugees. They were capable and indepen-dent individuals who needed opportunities, not handouts. This was something we realized only after we got to meet them for ourselves. They didn't look like what we had expected, and the encounter re-sulted in drastic changes in our projects. We lost a lot of sleep over our projects, mostly under the guidance of Ms. Lee, who also didn't get much sleep that week.

Despite our fatigue, we still perked up at the 'Leadership Com-munications' plenary session. Here Mr. Tarnowski taught us the art of speech writing. On the first day, we were given the homework of de-ciding our speech topic. The framework for our speeches was one cre-ated by a Harvard Kennedy School Professor and President Obama's speech coach, Marshall Ganz: 'The Story of Self, the Story of Us, the Story of Now.' Compared to the previous speech framework I had worked with, Aristotle's Pathos, Ethos and Logos, Professor Marshall Ganz's approach seemed a lot more organic, as it focused on emotions and connections and on telling a story. As Mr. Tarnowski said, 'To make them know what you know, you have to make them feel what you feel.'

On the second day, we met and pitched our speech topics, using those three components. All of my teammates, most of whom I had dismissed as non-contenders, had incredible stories that hit me hard: one of experiencing discrimination in something he loved and excelled in; one of constructive competitiveness and the drive to achieve; one of witnessing and experiencing extreme unwarranted pain from a protective figure. Hearing their experiences and their desires, only then did I understand the phrase 'we are made of stories.' Each individual had been formed by experiences that shaped their personalities, motivations and desires. The overall narrative of these interwoven factors created the stories that they shared in their speeches. Speechwriting is a skill often taught in cold, lifeless, literature terms: analogies, inclusive language, calls to action. At the ALY Camp, I finally connected the definition to the meaning and learned the power of that essence.

Now, you have to understand that beyond the speeches, we also had to work on our Refugee Project, build our personal brand and complete homework for our other two workshop sessions. Hence, despite not getting to sleep until around 4 a.m., my speech was very subpar and rough. On the other hand, the lack of a completely present consciousness when I was writing the speech prevented me from editing my work, and so the speech I made the next day was the raw, uncut, unedited word-vomit of my thoughts and emotions. I actually really enjoyed it. The lack of clearly scripted thought processes within it allowed me to focus less on what I was saying and more on connecting with the audience to convey my central message, which was 'the importance of conversation.' I kept only three things in mind:

my story, our story and now's story.

My story: I began with my rejection of human companionship in favor of stories, something similar to this chapter's introduction but more specific. I talked about how I would go to school and sit in the science block stairwell, alone with only the company of my chosen story, whenever I had free time, because books were more interesting to me than my classmates. I'd reject offers of card games, sports friendlies and plain companionship in order to be alone with my book or downloaded movie.

Our story: I talked about our recent experience at the ALY Camp, about meeting each other. I talked about our mini interview sessions and our night classes and finding out each other's stories, the pain in our pasts and our defining moments in life, our values, beliefs, motivations and dreams. I talked about how surprised we all were to find that each of us had an incredible story that none of the rest of us expected, how we all thought we were special in a sea of mediocrity. I talked about how easily the boundaries we put up could be broken down to connect us all, simply through talking.

Now's story: I talked of our increasingly globalized world, juxtaposed with our increasingly technologically divided lives. The globalized world and the need for communication and the understanding of others was a theme emphasized in our cross-cultural workshop. Given the world's many different cultures, open, engaging and deep communication has become more important than ever. How can we overcome strife and conflict if we ourselves have not made the effort to connect with and understand one another? As Mr. Tarnowski put it, 'It would be much harder to bomb Malaysia now that I've been here and I know that there's this great student named XYZ here.' Yet we have become so absorbed in our own universe, in our own stories, that we forget that everybody else is also a walking library of their own tales. They hold their personal, cultural and national stories—so many stories that we can learn from and immerse ourselves in.

After the ALY Camp, I watched a video by Vlogbrothers on the recent Comic Con. What the author John Green said in the video really tied everything together for me. He used a term called 'Cheetos Media' to represent our mindless consumption of media, which has become a common practice in my generation. There is so much media all around us, readily available and begging to be watched. There is always a new and hot hit, always a different one. I've had many conversations with equally if not more media obsessed friends, and I've found that if you debate media long enough, you'll eventually come to the same conclusion: we will never be able to consume all of it. It's not even a matter of the short duration of our lives; new media is produced faster than we can ever consume it. You will never reach the end of your read, watch or playlist. This may seem sad, but consider this: how many books have you read, how many movies have you watched, how many songs have you listened to that have left a lasting impression on you, and that you can still recall? If you compare this number to the amount you have consumed, the answer is not much.

Throughout the ALY Camp, the importance of conversation kept coming up—the need to communicate and connect with others around us in order to improve. Whether in business, leadership or just regular companionship, talking to one another was emphasized as the key to success. In addition to its being the logically correct course of action, I also noticed how much happier and supported it made me feel. I felt connected with everybody around me at the

ALY Camp: the other students, the Teaching Fellows, the Student Leaders and even the random people we passed between classes. All of this happened simply because I bothered to notice the people around me and actively wanted to engage with them. I realized that the difficulties and dragging weight I felt whenever I was thrown into a situation that required me to socialize were all in my mind. I had developed problems and obstacles where none existed. Attending the ALY Camp, where I was surrounded 24/7 by people I was required to socialize with, was something I used to equate with suffering. It took going through that experience to make me realize that every horror I associated with socializing was my own illusion, every suffocating social obligation a monster of my own creation.

As clichéd as it is, the ALY Camp gave me an epiphany, not suddenly but through collective experiences: stories come from people. It's an obvious realization but something I think we too often forget. Stories come from people, and 'people are made of stories.' I entered the ALY Camp with a lot of stuff (literally), and I left with even more: new friends, enlightening experiences, bright opportunities and a new view of the people around me. Yet I felt so much lighter than when I first walked in.

It's not just a temporary change either. Now, two weeks after leaving the ALY Camp, as I'm writing this, I've made it a life goal to connect with somebody new every day, whether it be the garbage man, the neighbor I've avoided meeting for the past ten years or a random person on the street when I walk my dog. So far, it hasn't been a complete success, but it's pretty close. Unread messages have turned into 'mamak' nights, something my friends may appreciate even more than I do. I've also made an effort to connect with and appreciate my family more, to be more aware of everything my parents have done for me and what they continue to do. I have to admit that this has been harder to overcome after living away from home for a year and given the generation gap. However, I'd like to think that my relationship with my parents has become closer than ever, despite our different opinions on certain issues. I love my family and friends dearly, and I'm now trying to express it a bit more often, because of what I've learned from the ALY Camp.

Now, whenever I build up sufficient trust of someone new, I love asking them questions that reveal their stories—questions I learned from the ALY Camp, such as, 'What was the turning point in your life?', 'What is your most memorable life moment?' or 'If you could convince the world of one thing, what would it be?' These are questions that hopefully will enable them to reveal their true selves. All in all, I've finally learned to love participating in conversations and reaching out to people from all walks of life. It's a precious activity that allows us to open our hearts, letting others in and creating joy in our lives.

| Chapter 3 |

Have Courage and Be Kind

Bryan Chay

● ● ●

A common topic in discussions with my peers and family members is our future plans. When my friends or younger relatives hear the question, 'What are you going to do when you leave school?' their responses are usually quick and assertive: "I want to go to ... and study ... and become a ... so that I can change the world by ..." My responses are much shorter: "I want go to university, but I'm still thinking on what to study." This is a lie. I've never really thought about my purpose in the world, apart from worshiping the Lord. I tend to feel stuck at a crossroad with no sense of direction. I have a couple of interests and goals, but they aren't concrete enough to help me make big decisions and identify my purpose in life.

Another problem I've faced is a lack of self-confidence. Growing up in a multicultural society and attending an international school in Kuala Lumpur, Malaysia, I've found that my fellow students position themselves according to social standards and a hierarchy of popularity.

People who are good at sports and are extroverted have lots of friends and are well-liked. I, on the other hand, have played a few sports but was never good enough to be chosen for a school team. I've made a couple of friends, but I've never had the courage to talk to strangers. Up to fourth grade I was content just studying—it didn't concern me that I was introverted because it didn't affect my grades or happiness most of the time—but now, understanding that connections with people are one of the most important tools of success, I've started to become more self-aware. This has had a domino effect not only on my grades but also on my self-confidence. Recently I developed a poor work ethic and lacked the ability to finish work on time. Usually I'd start off well, then take a break, leaving the rest of the work to the last minute or not finishing it at all. I needed help. I needed positive experiences to change my mindset.

'Harvard'—the word captured my and my parents' attention. Eagerly I signed up for the ALY Camp. We had heard that the course would be taught by Harvard alumni, using the same tools and technique that are used in the Ivy League university. It sounded fantastic. I wanted to gain a better sense of direction for my future and to improve my self-confidence through the group projects and, most notably, the speech competition. Simultaneously, I also wanted to work on 'developing a personal brand' both for myself and for others—e.g. universities, so that they can better understand and know my personality and goals. Finally, I hoped that the ALY Camp would increase my persistence and optimism, thus improving my sliding work ethic.

As I write this chapter, it has been two weeks since I stepped foot into the residence hall and prepared to introduce myself to my fellow roommates. As I inserted my key into the keyhole, my mind instructed me: *socialize, make friends, make all of this worthwhile*. I exhaled and practiced my smile two, three, ten times. Then I pushed the door open and was greeted by five friendly faces. I heard the same repeated story: 'My parents forced me to be here.' Eventually, I found myself lying on my bed, phone in my hand, scrolling through Facebook and thinking about the classes I would be attending in nine hours.

During the program, I was attracted to the 'Child Refugee Crisis' workshop. In the weeks prior to the program, I had kept abreast with updates on the refugee crisis. I learned that more and more refugee children are being abused and that no one is protecting them. During my last academic year, we participated in an after-school activity every Friday in which a long line of refugee children would come to our school. The students, usually in sixth form, would teach and play sports or games with the children. It was heartwarming to see such small deeds putting smiles on the children's faces. The students made the children feel loved and assured them that they mattered in this world; they took on the responsibility of bringing happiness to the kids. I didn't participate in this activity because I was caught up with lots of school work at the time. So when I discovered that now I could finally do something about the child refugee crisis myself, I jumped at the opportunity.

My second choice was the 'Introduction to Entrepreneurship' workshop. I am fascinated by the world of business, and I would like to learn how to be an entrepreneur and change the world by taking risks—as well as hopefully making a lot of money. Our task in the workshop was to create our own business plan and describe our idea in an elevator pitch. The activity trained me to think like a businessman, with a risk-taking and innovative mindset. My group and I came up with the idea of fitting carbon emissions filters into car exhausts to reduce emissions. It was fun but challenging at the same time, as we had to calculate the costs and propose a suitable price for our product.

My final choice was the 'Applying to U.S. Universities' workshop which I really enjoyed. During that class, Mr. Tarnowski gave us invaluable insights on applying to schools in the United States. I would like to study there primarily because of the vibrant and conducive learning environment its universities offer. The previous summer, I had the opportunity to visit a few campuses on the West Coast, and they were everything I had expected and more. I was fascinated by the college sports leagues and by the student culture there.

I found all of the classes exceptionally informative and enjoyable, thanks to the wonderful and down-to-earth teaching staff. I thoroughly enjoyed Ms. Lee's class using the case study method, which was completely new and refreshing. I learned to use the case framework, which encourages students to dissect a scenario into different sections—the protagonist, the current status, etc. Breaking the case down into its core components allows you to see a wider spectrum of possibilities and answers by allowing you to combine the elements into new and improved solutions. After completing the ALY Camp, I started to use her methods, and they have greatly enhanced my analytical skills, enabling me to look at carefully dissected segments instead of analyzing an entire situation at one go.

Another memorable topic was finding out our values and goals and how they can help us to achieve our purpose. It took me almost the whole week to figure that out. At first I was quite stressed out by the irritating feeling of not knowing what my goals and values were.

However, I was comforted by Ms. Lee's words, 'You're not going to know your purpose in one night.' The experience taught me something that I hadn't realized before that I feel blessed to have discovered now. I was stressing myself out for no reason. I was focusing on my weaknesses instead of improving my strengths. But eventually my weaknesses will balance out, and subsequently, I won't have a low overall standard.

I discovered that my strengths included selflessness and generosity, which enable me to be a 'giving' person. Opportunities soon arose for me to demonstrate these strengths. As my group and I were finishing our project on improving the refugee crisis, I offered to stay back and assist with completing the protest posters, working until 12:30 a.m. In doing so, I was able to talk to my group members and socialize with them. It made me realize that it wasn't so difficult getting to know new people. In fact, it was so enjoyable that I didn't even notice how late it was. The atmosphere became more vibrant, and I had a lot of fun working with my teammates, whom I now call friends. Our laughter echoed through the room as we started talking about comics and 'High School Musical.' One of my team members had an ostentatious and unique laugh, which no one could resist—not even me.

Family and friends. Two of the most crucial aspects of life that drive you and shape you. I wouldn't have made it through the program without them. At night, after all my classes and dinner, I never went to bed without calling my mother and telling her about my day—how hard things were, how much homework I still needed to finish or simply that I missed home. Every time, without fail, I would say good night and end the phone call with her feeling more motivated and happier than before. Then I would do my homework with my hilarious and friendly roommates.

One of the most interesting sessions I attended was led by Mr. Kim. He told us about one of his classmates from Harvard who had seen horrors in Mumbai, where he once witnessed a baby die in her mother's arms. Millions of these cases occur simply because incubation for premature babies is too expensive for many Indian mothers. Mr. Kim's friend envisioned saving millions of babies by creating an affordable but well-functioning incubator that didn't need electricity as a power source (something that raises the price). He was successful, and I was astonished by this man's achievement. I too would like to save lives, especially the lives of children. I want to become a pediatrician and practice medicine in the United States. Moreover, his story resonated with me for a special reason. I was not born prematurely, but I was admitted to the hospital with a potentially life-threatening illness around five years ago. I was diagnosed with dengue fever, and my pediatrician, who had been my family's doctor for ten years, took extremely good care of me. He showed me a different side of himself, a warm and caring side, and I have felt thankful to him ever since.

A few days after the ALY Camp, I thought about how I could change the world and make it a better place, even though I didn't have ideas for a life-changing invention. Mr. Tarnowski's class on 'Applying to U.S. Universities' taught us to include in our personal statement, not only how we will benefit but also how they will benefit from accepting us—in other words, we should explain what we can offer. Mr. Tarnowski's class helped me to understand myself; I realized that I want to pursue a career in pediatrics and apply kindness, self-lessness and generosity in the journey. Throughout the two weeks that have passed since I received my certificate of completion and participation in the ALY Camp, I have been pondering and attempting to come up with a medical breakthrough—and I have felt depressed at my failure. If I had not been able to speak to Ms. Lee about my 'mid-life crisis,' I would have been demotivated and distraught. But speaking to her calmed me because she led me to the realization that even a doctor who doesn't cure cancer can still make the world a better place merely by being one of the kindest, most selfless and most generous doctors out there. After our talk, I feel ready to face the world.

The intensive program pushed me to my limits in terms of workload and deadlines. Every night, I stayed up until midnight to finish long pieces of homework from the lessons of the day. The pressure forced me to cut off any distractions, including video games and social media, especially Facebook. I did this for seven nights in a row. Additionally, seeing people with such an incredible work ethic, both my fellow delegates and our teachers, motivated me to work harder than ever before, and this continued outside of the program. I saw a significant and drastic change in my everyday assignments.

At two points within the program, we had to break out of our shells and do something that was most definitely for me, out of my comfort zone. One of these activities was writing and delivering speeches on issues we felt passionate about, accompanied by personal anecdotes. I detest public speaking, and normally when an opportunity for public speaking arises, I am the first to decline it. However, after delivering my speech at the ALY Camp, I realized how uplifting it was: I felt as if I had accomplished a major goal. As it turned out, I did not dislike public speaking, I merely hated the thought of it. I had never considered the possibility that I might genuinely enjoy it.

The second activity was one of the most difficult and embarrassing for someone as self-conscious as I am. The Center for Asia Leadership Initiatives (CALI) partnered with Cyber Care, a non-profit organization that supports underprivileged children, including refugees, and gave us a chance to interact directly with the public. The theme was 'random acts of kindness.' We were split into five groups and decided on our chosen act of kindness. Then we went to a shopping mall and carried them out for strangers. This was by far one of the most difficult things I have ever had to do in public, especially since it looked as if we were selling something. Our initial plan of free hugs didn't work, since people in Malaysia are not used to hugging strangers. We then decided to go for a lighter and easier approach: free high fives. It worked a lot better. At one point, my shoulder actually felt numb from holding up my arm to receive so many high fives. Soon we started offering compliments to passers-by as well. I feel that this exercise, challenging though it was, allowed me to be brave and confident and helped me to improve my social skills.

'It is like a mustard seed, which is the smallest of all seeds on earth. Yet when planted, it grows and becomes the largest of all garden plants, with such big branches that the birds can perch in its shade' (Mark 4:31-32). My learning experience from this program relates well to this Bible verse. To me, it means that no matter who you are or how small you may think your purpose is, you don't need to panic. Instead, be courageous and work hard, and create your own nourishing environment. Only then you can plant yourself in the world and watch your own potential grow into something great. At that point, the birds—your wife, girlfriend, father, mother, siblings, friends, and other people in need of help—can admire you and perch under your leaves.

I am very grateful for the opportunity to have met and worked with the amazing Harvard alumni and wonderful people at the ALY Camp. I will never forget this life-changing experience. The course has done wonders for me, and I am ready to plant myself and face the world.

| Chapter 4 |

Taking Small Steps

Jonson Tham

●●●

At some point in our lives, we all have to step out of our comfort zones and hope for the best—even if it is something we think we don't want. When we take this leap of faith, we just might get something great out of it, something we never expected. In my case, it happened from July 11-16, 2016, during my sweet summer break. I did not choose to be part of the experience—it was my parents' decision. But I am forever thankful for that decision.

I came home from school one day, tired from my afternoon activities. Sinking into the sofa, I flipped through the entertainment section of the newspaper. Then my mom plopped down beside me on the sofa. "Son," she told me, "I'm signing you up for the ALY Camp!" That was the start of a journey I never expected. Before I participated in the ALY Camp, I would have said that I was just an average guy in secondary school, one who was not very confident about himself. I always thought I was the blunt knife in the midst of the many sharp ones around me. I felt overlooked by everyone. To hide my insecurities, I cracked jokes to make people laugh, so that I could feel better about myself, even though I soon realized that it didn't really get me anywhere. Things changed when I took part in the ALY Camp. I learned to accept myself and discovered that I should feel proud of who I am, no matter what others think. I am not just a hollow shell filled with emptiness but rather a balloon, filled with personality and capabilities that will slowly but surely grow bigger with each passing day. The ALY Camp taught me not only how to be a leader but also how to understand myself first before leading others.

Many fun activities were held during the ALY Camp. My favorites were the ones related to discovering our true personalities. In Mr. Kim's 'Building a Successful Personal Brand and Building a Successful Career Path,' I partook in an exercise that required me to write down whatever I wanted on my tombstone. The activity encouraged us to think about our contributions during our time on earth and what kind of legacy we wished to leave behind when the time comes. Personally, I wanted to be remembered as a very motivated person who could keep his cool in times of hardship. I wrote, 'Here lies the man who put on a happy face at times when others were sad.' This simple sentence was enough to represent the kind of person I wanted to become. Mr. Kim's class also allowed us to take a personality test, and that was the activity I enjoyed most. We had to answer over two hundred questions in order to get accurate results. The test opened up my eyes to my weaknesses and strengths, as well as to potential careers in the future. It was the most interesting session for me during the ALY Camp. The information I gained was both captivating and useful for my future plans. I would like to thank Mr. Kim for giving me the chance to unearth that information.

I also particularly enjoyed Mr. Panche Kralev's 'Authentic Leadership' class, in which I had to rate the activities I liked from highest to lowest. The results showed that I could be compared to an otter, meaning a leader who always cheers his team on and motivates them in a fun manner. The class gave me a lot of pointers on how I can best lead my team with my own personality, as well as identifying my weaknesses.

The night activities were very entertaining and enjoyable. They all taught one universal theme, that there is no 'I' in team. To succeed, we had to work together to achieve a common goal. A person with more experience should be the one who leads the others step by step, so that the others can one day reach the level of the leader. We can do anything if we work together. The night activities that required the most teamwork were captain ball and ice skating. In captain ball, we all worked in a team and acted as our own leaders, giving opportunities to handle the ball to those who were better at it, but also allowing those who were not as skillful to handle the ball too, in order to hone their skills. The result was a tie, but we managed to win the match in the end, thanks to our collaborative effort! Before the ALY Camp, I hadn't realized how difficult ice skating was. It requires a lot of skill and balance, which all of us lacked because it was the first for most of us. We fell down so many times that I was surprised we didn't break the ice! Ice skating demands a lot of hard work, and I found it difficult to master the basics. However, with a little teamwork and cooperation, we managed to skate several times around the rink, which wasn't bad for a first timer like myself, even though I fell eight times. Hitting the ice was an uncomfortable feeling, as it was colder than

Antarctica and froze my senses—but at least we survived!

The key lesson from the ALY Camp was that I must be confident and should always believe, respect and love myself. The ALY Camp was designed in such a way that we could fully utilize the skills and knowledge we acquired from the Teaching Fellows, who helped us to go out there and apply what we learned in a real setting. For example, we participated in a workshop that involved critical thinking on how to provide a solution to the refugee crisis in Malaysia. Through this case-in-point project and a surprising community service exercise, I was able to overcome my lack of confidence and respect for myself.

All of us engaged in the community service exercise, which required us to carry out random acts of kindness. As preparation, we created cards and flyers to distribute to shoppers at Sunway Pyramid, one of the largest malls in Malaysia. I helped my group look up some nice pickup lines and wrote them down on pieces of paper that we then decorated. We were assigned the area in front of a hypermarket, near a fancy automobile display. I took my signs and walked around the area with the group, telling people nice things and trying to get them to accept our flyers. Our main goal was to spark an inviting feeling in order to make people feel welcome, hoping that they might then spread the word of kindness to others. However, it was hard at first to convince the shoppers to accept our flyers. Then we had an idea. I went to shop for some sweets with one of my group members, Benjamin Woo. It was fun handing out sweets to kids who passed by and offering flyers to their parents. Eventually, the mall visitors began to warm up to our actions. The activity taught me that community service is a noble effort that can benefit every level of society. But there is a far greater message: community service teaches us how it feels to get rejected and how to relate that feeling to the times when we have refused to listen or accept other people's efforts to promote their products or causes. It is not easy work. Although we knew that most people would probably turn a blind eye to our efforts, we kept going until we finally achieved our goal. No matter how polite or nice we were, some people still refused to take the flyers, and sometimes people were rude to us. We were exhausted by the end of the day, but it taught me that gratitude and kindness can put smiles on people's faces.

Once my group and I were back at the ALY Camp, we were introduced to Kitti, a humanitarian worker who has been doing work for the refugees in Malaysia. She told us to gather around and asked about our ALY Camp experience. There was a lot of different answers, but most of them were positive. She then encouraged each of us to share our experiences with the rest of the delegates. I decided to give it a shot, since it was my last day and I was feeling quite energetic. What I didn't know was how different reality would be, compared to what I expected.

I started off talking about being an insecure person; I made some jokes about myself and described myself as 'the crazy guy going around and asking people to smile,' which, sure enough, got some laughs from the audience. After sharing my whole experience, I expected Kitti to ask me about what I had learned that day. I had prepared to say that we have to treat others well in order for them to accept us. That was when the unexpected happened.

Instead of asking me what I had hoped to answer, she said, 'Do you mind if I get a little personal with you?' That shocked me—the whole thing seemed to be taking a wrong turn. But I agreed. It may sound like a mistake at that moment, but what she asked actually made me open up about my true self. Her question was simple yet complicated: 'Are you usually the leader of the group or just the one who stands behind?'

I was stunned. I didn't know the answer to this question, nor did I realize how bad I had made myself sound when I shared my experience. I had never really thought about it—all I wanted were laughs and jokes, but now I know that making fun of yourself isn't worth a positive response from your audience. It just shows that you don't respect yourself and that you're not confident or comfortable with yourself.

'Both, but usually the leader,' I answered.

'Then, why were you not the one asking other people for hugs?'

Again I was dumbfounded. I'm not sure what I said at that time because I was so busy thinking about the question. All I felt was disappointment as Kitti's comments made me open up my mind and think about myself. I wondered, 'Is this who I really am, someone who wants to hide in the shadows of others, making fun of himself just to feel a little better? Is this who I was raised to be? Was this why I attended this ALY Camp, just to let all my insecurities drag me down again?'

Suddenly Kitti asked the crowd, 'How many of you think Jonson is huggable?' Without a moment of hesitation, many hands went up, with more and more shooting up as the seconds passed. Then my friend Nicholas Yang stood up, walked toward me and embraced me in a warm hug. Upon seeing that, a whole group of guys I had come to know during the ALY Camp stood up and gave me a gigantic group hug. It felt like warm ocean breeze flowing through my body, a mass of radiance shining upon me. I felt their trust, compassion and warmth. But most of all, I felt hope. I felt the confidence they gave me, a force so strong that it broke the barriers that had been hiding deep within my soul this whole time. I felt myself breaking free, being able to open myself up without having to fear judgements anymore. It was the best feeling in the world.

When it ended, I didn't know how to react. I felt deeply touched that so many people believed in me, even though I didn't know them well. I looked down, thinking of what I had been missing out all this time, just because I tried to hide who I am. I wasn't taught to be insecure or unconfident or to let my weaknesses drown me in sorrow. Instead, I was taught to rise to the challenge and knock down all the barriers that prevent me from showing the world who I truly am.

A voice brought me back to reality: 'Seeing the way you're looking down, I'm assuming you're trying to take it all in?' Yes, I certainly was, but those were not the words that came out of my mouth. Instead I faced the crowd, looking at each and every person I had gotten to know over the past six days, and said, 'Thank you.' I made some jokes after that, and we all laughed. Then it was time to return to my seat. This memory will forever etched in my heart.

Soon it was time for the graduation dinner, in which all of us would receive our hard-earned certificates and reunite with our parents. It also meant that we would have to say goodbye to each other. Well, all good things must come to an end. I chatted with the other delegates, and we asked each other about leaving the ALY Camp. Everyone agreed that we would dearly miss the experience as well as the people we had met. I joked around with my roommates, saying it would be a relief not to live with Linus anymore—he was one of my roommates and liked turning the air conditioning on full blast when he slept. Our room felt like a freezer at night!

Later in the evening, some of the delegates went on stage to deliver their speeches. One of the delegates, Ruben, gave a speech that truly inspired me. It was about stepping out of your comfort zone because only by doing so can you achieve your full potential. He described how he had always been comfortable in his own bubble. Fear always got the better of him every time he wanted to take up a challenge. But he refused to succumb to fear and went on to become the head prefect of his school, as well as representing his school in public speaking for various events. He had even been voted the best public speaker numerous times. I was really amazed by his achievements. There and then, I vowed to accomplish greater things in life!

After leaving the ALY Camp, I began to notice some changes in me. I am more confident now, and I'm not afraid to step out of my comfort zone and try things I was scared to do before. I started taking small steps to change. First, I began wearing a wristband to school. I have small wrists, and they look funny if I wear wristbands, but I don't care anymore if my friends judge me for it. Then I decided to join more competitions, including swimming and tae kwon do. It doesn't matter if I win or lose—what matters is that I must try my best in everything I do. By stepping out of my comfort zone, I will interact with more people and learn more about their backgrounds and lifestyles, which will strengthen our bonds. These are small actions, but they are effective all the same. I have promised myself to go out of my way to acquire new knowledge and gain more life experience. I encourage all of you to step out of your comfort zones too and start doing the things you've always wanted to do. The first step is the beginning of your journey to success.

I hope to inspire all the readers out there with my story. I would like everyone to know that each of us is unique in our own way. Brush away any insecurities you may have and feel proud of who you are. Break down barriers and be the change that you want in this world. Take risks to get where you want to in life. If you are not sure where that is, then jump into the unknown with open arms. Take the leap of faith. Wherever you end up going, it is bound to be a great adventure. If it is not, then take another turn, and another, and another, until you reach your destination. Life has unexpected turns, yet they wield many astonishing surprises. There will be people who think you're not good enough, but bear in mind that these people criticize you because they are afraid of stepping out of their own comfort zones. Don't let the naysayers drag you down. Always stand strong, but with others, not above them. You are here on earth for a reason. Carve your own path and inspire others to live life to the fullest.

Chapter 5

My Life-Changing Experience

Ben Ang Zi Qi

● ● ●

'I want to join this program!' was what the voice in my head exclaimed during the preview of the ALY Camp. I was an eighteen-year-old teenage boy, totally clueless and with no sense of direction, until the day of the preview, which was when I saw light. To be frank, it was the first time in my life I voluntarily chose to join a leadership camp. As a result of my decision, I was able to meet the wonderful Teaching Fellows of Harvard and was given an opportunity to learn from the content and experiences they shared.

When I was twelve, my father forced me to join a motivational course, as he was hoping I would turn over a new leaf and show more interest in my studies. I shut myself inside my comfort zone and pretended to participate in the camp's activities, but I ended up returning home with almost zero knowledge from the course. Only when I was fourteen, after attending several trainings to groom myself as a future coach for Adam Khoo Learning Technologies Group, did I finally open my eyes. It was my first time stepping out of my comfort zone, and I participated fully in the activities, with enough drive to be selected as their coach. It took me seven attempts to get selected for the first time, but my determination and perseverance paid off in the end. Being able to change other people's lives for the better is definitely something I enjoy doing. It gave my life purpose, yet I was unsure if it was the best option for me. I knew I was still unprepared to tackle future challenges, and this was why I made the decision to join the ALY Camp. I hoped that I would be able to acquire better communication skills, such as the art of persuasion, as well as better listening and thinking skills.

Throughout the program, I got to mingle with people from many different backgrounds and made a lot of new friends. Almost all the activities involved group work. Many of you may wonder why, and I asked myself the same question on the first day, but I soon realized the true meaning behind this group work. Ms. Lee, the Teaching Fellow of the Entrepreneurial Leadership Plenary Session, emphasized collaboration by providing every group with Post-It notes during group activities and discussions. Each delegate was required to write down as many ideas as possible and post them on the group's flip-charts. It was very unlike regular discussions, in which the extroverts of the group spit out most of the ideas while the introverts keep their thoughts hidden deep in their minds. By spouting ideas this way, each group member was able to share his or her point of view without stopping other members from sharing theirs. Before the end of the session, we were given five minutes to categorize and reorganize our ideas. It was messy but resulted in a fruitful outcome, as we looked at the bigger picture and started working toward the optimal idea.

Moreover, it was often truly shocking to read other group members' ideas because it made you ask yourself, 'I know that! Why didn't that come to mind?' Sometimes, the ideas provided by my peers were alien to me but still rational and feasible. I absorbed a lot of ideas from them, and I learnt that even if the same problem is given to everyone in a group, each person will approach the situation differently and will produce different solutions to obtain the end result. Hence, the opinions of each group member are valuable, and it is unwise to ignore them.

Mr. Kim taught us about building a powerful personal brand. He began by telling us his story: he was aimless; he had no idea what he wanted to do after graduating and switched jobs more than six times. However, he had two clear goals that gave him the drive to reach the point where he is today: one was to make a lot of money, and the other was to lend a helping hand to people who are in need. When he was our age, he left Korea for the Philippines with his parents, who were humanitarian aid workers. They did not earn much, but it was enough to support the family and to help people in need. Since then, he has committed himself to working hard in order to support his family, so that they can live a comfortable life and help others as well. He told us that we were lucky to have so much support from our parents, our school teachers and those peers who are more experienced than we are and are willing to share their knowledge with us. Mr. Kim also looks up to Abraham Lincoln and wants to emulate his success. Abraham Lincoln was the sixteenth President of the United States, and he ended slavery through sheer determination. Lincoln believed and trusted his subordinates even though rumors suggested that they were planning a revolution against him, and this trust is one of the characteristics that Mr. Kim admires most.

Mr. Kim encouraged us to think of buzzwords and logos that represent ourselves and how we want others to see us. His buzzword was 'stepping stone' because he wants to help as many people as possible, giving others a head start by sharing his experiences with them and helping them to realize their dreams early, so that they can be prepared for challenges in the near future. I, on the other hand, chose 'caring,' as I always think of others first and feel the need to help them. At college, I will always hold the door for everyone, including friends, lecturers and strangers. If a friend has left his or her valuables in class, I will inform them immediately and return their belongings in our next class. I am always there for my family whenever they need me, and I cherish their love and support. This is why I chose the buzzword 'caring' to reflect my personality.

Every country has its own unique culture, which differs from those of other nations across the globe. 'Cross-Cultural Competencies,' conducted by Teaching Fellow Mr. Tarnowski, was the most enjoyable workshop I attended. Mr. Tarnowski was enthusiastic and always interested in our thoughts and ideas. The class made you ask yourself, 'How much do I actually know about my culture and others'?' Culture is not something you can understand instantly, just as Rome was not built in a day. In order to understand a culture, you have to live with it and apply it in your daily life. During the workshop, we participated in a role-playing session in which we were split into two groups, the first group acting as the Hokies and the second group Heelotians. Hokies are people who value quantity over quality, and they are very open. Heelotians are the opposite: they prefer quality to quantity and are self-centered. If you lay even a finger on them, they will hiss at you and run away.

Our objective as a group was to gather information from the other group through interaction with its citizens. Both groups were first given a few minutes to observe each other's culture, and then the High Heelot and the High Hokie, the leaders of the respective tribes, each selected two negotiators to visit the other tribe. Funny and frustrating were two words to describe the activity, but we enjoyed ourselves as we did our best to complete our quest. My comrades and I were Heelotians, and we had a hard time with the Hokies, as the High Hokie tricked us into committing 'offences' in their culture in order to punish us. Meanwhile, the High Heelot was willing to help the clueless Hokie negotiators by providing them with hints about our culture.

Applying the simulation to the real world, we realized that the frustrations of cultural interactions are true worldwide. If you observe another culture without living in it, you will see only the tip of the iceberg. Moreover, different individuals in the same culture may treat you differently, even if they perform similar practices. For example, if I were to enter a foreign land knowing nothing about its culture, the locals might alienate me and not entertain me, or they might try to help me find my way around, or even both.

My country, Malaysia, is a melting pot of cultures, with people from a range of backgrounds. Diversity is our strength, and we are usually able to accept each other despite our differences. Together, we create a truly Malaysian identity.

Pre-independence Malaysia was known as Malaya. The British separated the three main races, namely the Malays, Chinese and Indians, under their 'divide and rule' policy. They believed that a segregated Malaya would prevent the colonized people from uniting to retaliate.

The British also believed that each race should be put to work according to its abilities, which led to separate economies segregated by race. After the Second World War, Malaya's native political leaders, especially Onn Ja'afar, realized that unity was crucial in seeking independence. Onn left the United Malays National Organization (UMNO), the country's largest political party and that emphasized the aspirations of Malay nationalism, after his recommendation to open its doors to all races was dismissed by party members. He then founded the Independence of Malaya Party (IMP), but this new party failed to receive sufficient support from the locals, and Onn eventually left it to form Parti Negara.

Before becoming Malaysia's first Prime Minister, Tunku Abdul Rahman predicted that Onn's party would not survive after three months, as very few Malays had joined his party despite the membership of influential Chinese and prominent Indians. Tunku believed that the people of Malaya could not be united under a single political party. He stated that each community needed its own political party and leaders. Accordingly, he formed the Alliance Party, also known as Parti Perikatan before it was renamed Barisan Nasional, which consists of the UMNO, the Malayan Chinese Association (MCA), and the Malayan Indian Congress (MIC). The alliance won many votes and the people's support. It brought together people from the three major races and other ethnic groups as well.

Throughout the years, the accusations of racism in Malaysia have stemmed from the racial preferences manifest within the country's social and economic policies. Although racism in the country has greatly reduced over the years, some factors may still give foreigners the perception of a racist Malaysia. For example, we still have Malay, Chinese and Tamil vernacular schools, but, crucially, students from different races study in each of these schools. There are Malays studying in Chinese schools, Chinese students in Tamil schools and Indians attending Malay schools, though not many. I believe we can increase the number of students from diverse backgrounds in each school by deliberately enrolling our children in vernacular schools or national schools that differ from our own ethnic backgrounds. We can also organize exchange programs between vernaculars schools to allow students to mingle and make friends with other students who do not share their religion or beliefs. Vernacular schools could even forge partnerships and co-organize events, such as a sports day.

Food from many different cultures is a huge part of the Malaysian tradition. My country is well known for its wide variety of mouth-watering cuisines, such as *nasi lemak*, *roti canai* and *char kway teow*, which originated from the Malay, Indian and Chinese cultures respectively. These dishes are enjoyed not only by the locals but by foreign tourists as well! Another unique aspect of Malaysian culture is that we all speak at least two languages, namely English and Bahasa Malaysia, and many people also speak Tamil and Mandarin. It is not surprising to hear two friends from different races conversing in different languages and dialects within the same sentence. This ability is something to be proud of, and we feel blessed to be able to learn many languages. Learning them also helps us pick up other languages later in life. For example, Japanese is easy to learn if you know Mandarin, as Kanji uses Chinese characters.

At the ALY Camp, we were given the chance to experience what it's like to be as blind as a bat, in an activity called 'Dialogue in the Dark.' We were taken to a room with no light. Devices that can emit light were not allowed into the zone. Our tour guide, Michelle, was visually impaired herself, yet she was able to locate us and escorted us through the dark just by listening to our voices and relying on her other senses. Without our sight, it was very difficult for us to carry out simple tasks, such as climbing stairs, buying vegetables in the market and paying the bill. After forty-five minutes in total darkness, I felt guilty about stressing my precious eyes by staying up late and looking at a bright screen for long hours. Our eyes' lenses cannot regenerate, and damage once done stays throughout our lifetime. So bear in mind to protect your eyes and treat them carefully. I am very thankful to have a pair of healthy eyes, and this experience made me even more determined to do good for my community. Simple things like seeing enable me to learn and gain knowledge. I promise to study hard to become a man of worth and value. Being healthy helps me to do this and to achieve anything I aim for in life.

The theme of our community service was refugees, and members from the United Nations High Commissioner for Refugees (UN-HCR) were invited to give us a talk on the topic, which gave us a better understanding of the situation during the preparation stage. Learning that refugees are being treated unfairly and are often put on the same boats as illegal immigrants saddened me because many of them left their country of birth as a result of war or political issues. As if that were not heartbreaking enough, they are often unable to pursue their dreams because they are not given educational rights in the countries they take refuge in.

After the talk, we engaged in a brainstorming exercise to come up with a problem statement and solutions for the session. We asked the UNHCR members for feedback on our recommendations. Personally, I thought we should focus on tackling the language barrier and urging the government to act by amending their policies and allowing refugees to gain access to education. Our group decided that the language barrier and the lack of teaching staff were the problems that most needed to be tackled. Many of the refugees in Malaysia cannot communicate in English because they speak only their mother tongue. It is thus hard for them to learn new skills because they need to understand English first. There is also a shortage of teaching staff, as most of the people who teach the refugees are either volunteers or lowly paid. The inability of educators to speak the refugees' languages also contributes to the insufficient number of teachers. We proposed solutions that were mostly similar to what UNHCR has already attempted to carry out but could not do so because of their policies. Our idea was to gather well-educated refugees to teach the younger refugees, since they would be able to break the language barrier and impart their knowledge to those who are hungry to learn.

Following the group presentations on the refugee issue, we were assigned to brighten up some strangers' days. It was an opportunity for us to break out of our comfort zones by pushing ourselves to offer acts of kindness. We gave away a lot of free high-fives, free hugs and free compliments to everyone who walked by. This also allowed us to understand the real world. Sometimes we were rejected by strangers, as some of them did not see our offerings as beneficial. Some even told us off that they thought we were doing something immoral. However, we also met kind people who wanted to take photos with us and accepted our 'gifts.' As for me, I exchanged many high-fives and gave tight hugs. Seeing the smiles on the strangers' faces made my day brighter. Many were also interested in the activity and wanted to know more about the ALY Camp! We completed the activity feeling tired but happy that our efforts had managed to touch others.

The ALY Camp ended with a graduation ceremony. I was one of the delegates who took the floor to share our experiences throughout the one-week program. I did my best to maintain eye contact with the audience as I spoke, and I even exchanged a high-five with a parent before ending my speech. My peers were excited and gave me a round of applause as I applied what we had learned in my presentation. I was glad that I had stepped up to the plate and grabbed the opportunity to communicate with a large audience. When I was twelve, I had missed a chance to speak in front of a crowd, but this time I took up the challenge without any hesitation.

To my friends who are reading this, I would like to tell you that no matter who you are, you have the potential to change the world if you are committed to doing so. Find your purpose in life before it is too late, because you will be aimless if you do not and your time will be invested in an inefficient way. I would like to thank Mr. Kim, for giving me the golden opportunity to contribute this book chapter, and everyone who was involved in the ALY Camp—Teaching Fellows, Student Leaders, Operation Team and delegates. Without all of you, this program would not have existed. Last but not least, thank you to my readers for taking the time to 'hear' me out, and I hope that you will achieve everything you wish for in life.

Chapter 6

Lessons I Didn't Learn in School

Kamaleshwaran Ganeson

● ● ●

'Who wouldn't want to be famous and have their own perspective about an experience documented in a book and published worldwide?' This was the first thought that came into my mind when I heard from Mr. Kim, President of the Center for Asia Leadership Initiatives (CALI), encouraging contributions from us campers regarding our experiences during the ALY Camp, hosted by CALI. It was supposed to be an essay about something we had learned or experienced, and I was instantly put into a dilemma: I had too much to say, since I had been through something that taught me so much, in such a short amount of time.

We all constantly strive to learn and become better while making a ton of mistakes along that path. However, as bad as those mistakes may be, they also come with valuable life lessons, which mold us into better people. Aside from mistakes, being able to reflect on our personal experiences tends to result in us learning more about ourselves.

So as I was reflecting on my experiences during the ALY Camp, I got a sudden burst of inspiration to shortlist some of the most prominent life lessons that had affected me, to share with the rest of the world. Someone else could definitely benefit from what I had learned, I was sure.

It was the night before the official start of the program, and all the participants had to check into their rooms and attend a short orientation to get a grasp of what they would be doing in the upcoming week. Before the program started, we had to settle down in our rooms. Reaching my dorm room, I went in and found two of my roommates, one whom I already knew from college. We were surprised to find each other there, and the conversation flowed easily. The new guy I met was nice too, and we hit it off.

The three of us were early for the program briefing, so the conversation kept going as people began to fill the hall. I saw new faces that I would be calling 'friends' sometime soon, and it was exciting and nerve-wrecking at the same time. The briefing then began, followed by the orientation activity, which required us to play a simple game and say one fact about ourselves as an introduction to the group. I had planned so many things to say, to make my first impression really good and friendly, so that people would want to be friends with me, but I ended up mumbling something about liking dogs, when in reality I don't even own any pets. 'Great job, genius. You had one job!' I chided myself. The first impression I made on the rest of the group was less than amazing, by my own standards. The main message I want to put forth is that sometimes in life we have to impress the people around us to gain an opportunity that might be invaluable, and we usually get only a single shot at it.

Later in the week, we learned about making elevator pitches. We practiced impressing all our friends and the Teaching Fellows, and during the practice session we discovered how vital it is to make a lasting and accurate impression on someone in the short time-span of one minute. Given this time pressure, it is best to focus on putting your best foot forward most of the time, as you never know when such a situation might arise.

In my case, the first chance I had to make an impression on my yet-to-be-friends went horribly, and I was sure that I would not be able to redeem myself after that monumental slip-up. However, I reasoned that if I wanted to give a better impression, make more friends and leave a lasting impact on these people I had just met, it was up to me to think and act in a certain way to ensure that it happened. I wasn't going to sit around, accepting that I had messed up an opportunity and thinking it was my only opportunity. Second chances are presented to us in the subtlest of ways, and sometimes it is up to us to venture out and create those second chances for ourselves. I spent the following days showcasing myself and my personality in all the activities, to show everyone the kind of person I am so that I could actually make friends. I participated in group projects, led my team for some activities, shared opinions and personal stories in discussions and even participated in the speech competition. At first I was hesitant, thinking that my participation and enthusiasm would be seen as distracting and over-the-top, in contrast to how everyone else would be. However, seeing that everyone else was equally enthusiastic, I grew even more excited to meet new people and make new friends.

All in all, I ensured that my name and presence would leave an impact in the lives of most of the campers who participated in the program. I wanted to find like-minded people to share my life journey with, so that we could inspire, motivate and propel each other to achieve great success in our lives and bring forth a great change in the world. I'd like to think that my mission was a success, but it would not have been so if I'd decided to sit back and accept my failed first attempt as my only chance. Opportunity seldom knocks twice, so make a door and open it for yourself instead. It will definitely be worth it. I can testify to that. By the end of the ALY Camp, I had made friends with all of the participants, even the Harvard Teaching Fellows and their Student Leaders. Mission accomplished!

'If you never try, you'll never know.' Coldplay is my favorite band, and these lyrics make a lot of sense in many situations, including my own experience at the end of my second day at the ALY Camp. After a great day of learning new concepts and gaining more knowledge through workshops and plenary sessions, it was time to unwind with the other delegates by playing a few rounds of a competitive sport— captain ball. I have never played the game before and was apprehensive about it, as I am not physically fit and always feel that other people are better at sports than I am. With my natural predisposition not to participate too much, I gravitated toward being a 'bencher' (a reserved or replacement player) instead of actively participating, but my teammates insisted that I be the 'catcher,' since I was the tallest and biggest in the group. At first I refused: I have butter fingers, and I knew I would just let the ball slip and cost our team serious points. I didn't want to be the one who let the entire team down; that kind of embarrassment and guilt would eat me up inside. Still, I ended up being the catcher in the end.

We started off well, but I had a hard time catching anything at all. I even missed easy shots and passes, costing us valuable points. Eventually, I swapped with someone else and stood by the sidelines, watching and cheering my team on. Some of my teammates began to get tired and wanted to take a break, but they couldn't because there were no replacements. There and then, I realized that I was being selfish, pulling out just because I didn't want to fail and disappoint my teammates. At that moment, I saw a teammate gasping for air, unable to keep up with the game. I felt an urgent need to help him and let go of my inhibitions, replacing him, I returned to the game, this time as a defender. I was determined to make my team proud. I knew I was not a great player, nor a great sportsman. I knew I would probably lose. But I didn't care anymore; I just wanted to make sure my friend got the rest he needed, and I decided to enjoy the game and not take it too seriously. In the end, we lost, but everyone had fun, including me. All that sweat I shed, playing a few rounds straight without switching with another teammate, was worth it. And what really made my day was when a teammate commented on how good I was and said I had the potential to be a pretty good defender in an actual captain ball team.

The lesson I learned here was never to let your assumptions get the best of you and limit your potential. I learned to live not in my head, which was filled with disruptive thoughts and assumptions, but in the moment, cherishing every second of it. Often, we rush to meet deadlines and place undue stress on ourselves, losing sight of the essence of life. We overlook certain issues and choose to remain ignorant, assuming that they are beyond our sphere of control or influence. Due to this sort of thinking, many opportunities slip right through our fingertips. If I had continued to assume that I was useless to my team and hadn't tried at all, I would have felt horrible once the game ended, besides feeling left out and guilty for not giving my teammates a chance to take a break when they were tired. I wouldn't have forged a stronger bond with my teammates, I wouldn't have discovered my potential as a good player and I wouldn't have surprised myself by enjoying a competitive sport. Even though playing a sport is totally out of my comfort zone, it was still a valuable experience—the more so since I discovered that I actually possess some potential to be good at it. Too often we limit ourselves by giving excuses to get back into our comfort zone and refusing to face any challenges. Take a chance and do something you never thought you would do, and the results may surprise you. Escape your comfort zone and break your mental barriers. Venture into the unknown and tap into your full potential. Never give up before you give it a go; because if you never try, you'll never know!

The main goal of any leadership program is to instill leadership qualities in its participants, encouraging them to take action and be leaders. However, many of these programs actually fail to do so because of a very simple reason: the participants have yet to understand or even know themselves. During a week-long plenary session held by Mr. Kim, he focused on the importance of building personal brands as well as getting to know ourselves as people in the process.

When Mr. Kim's sessions started on the first day, I was interested to find out what we would be working on. However, after his introduction to what we would be doing for the entire week—a lot of self-reflective exercises that required us to look back at ourselves and our lives—I felt quite apprehensive. This feeling is normal, as most Malaysian students dislike any activities that involve what they feel, their personal experiences and their own lives. Our apprehension is largely due to the fact that most of us are brought up with a very objective and work-oriented mind set, in which abstract concepts such as what we feel are not prioritized in comparison with other skills.

Nevertheless, I brushed aside those thoughts and decided to embrace an optimistic outlook on the activity, since valuable knowledge shared by someone of Mr. Kim's stature would definitely be beneficial. Most of his sessions were held as discussions in large groups, pairs or even individual reflective exercises. The sessions encouraged us to improve ourselves by showcasing our unique personalities. We discussed our role models and analyzed how great leaders of our time suffered drawbacks and hardships, yet still managed to reach their current positions. We even got a sneak peek into Mr. Kim's own journey of self-discovery. I felt inspired; I began wanting to discover more about myself and how I could be a great leader in the future, and I started thinking more about how to achieve that goal. However, I still felt a slight lack of direction—I missed a sense of purpose in life, besides just 'trying to make a difference.'

In the middle of the week, we were asked to come up with a buzzword: a word or short phrase that could be used to describe us, as well as what we strive to be or do with our lives. It needed to be a word that accurately described our aspirations in life and our unique personality, a word that would guide us toward refining and achieving whatever goal we set our sights on. I spent countless hours trying to figure something out for myself, but to no avail. I just couldn't figure out what described me in such a way that would also indicate my goal in life. Then I had a fateful encounter with a newfound friend at the ALY Camp. She helped me identify what my goals were and what I wanted to be in life, as well as assessing the type of person I am through her own observations. With her help, I stumbled across a word that fit me and my aspirations perfectly: 'canvas.' We use canvases to paint and create masterpieces. I want to be a canvas for all the painters out there who lack the proper outlet to express their ideas, thoughts and opinions. I want to be the one whom they look up to in their quest to achieve greatness. I want to make a difference by being there for people who need the support. Moreover, it is an apt word choice, as 'canvas' correlates with my desire to be an educator in the future.

The moral of this life-changing incident is not singular but plural. From just one encounter, I managed to learn several lessons about people and, most importantly, myself. I learned that apprehension and a natural predisposition to remain at the status quo, while fearing the unknown, does not lead to personal growth, only stagnancy. I also learned that gaining life experiences by having a role model not only boosts people's confidence but also inspires them to take the first steps toward a better life. I now understand the importance of teamwork and participating in group discussions: they provide us with the opportunity to look at things in a different way and to learn more about ourselves at the same time. The key takeaway from this experience is the nature of our role in becoming change agents and making a difference in the world. It is imperative to understand yourself. Only then can you identify your strengths and weaknesses, which will in turn help you to set your personal goals and unlock your full potential. No leader became great without knowing who he or she was. Leaders have a strong sense of self-awareness and a striking personal brand. So get to know yourself and watch the opportunities unfold in front of you.

Students can be a whiny bunch. It is normal to hear them complain about studying and having too much homework, assignments and projects. 'Studying is pointless, it's not for me' or 'Why study things that are not useful for my future?' These are just some of the statements that we usually come across. I wish to share a story on this topic.

Ms. Lee conducted the Design Thinking Challenge. We were put into separate groups and told to come up with a solution for the education problems faced by refugee children in our country. We went through a series of intense discussions, developing a systematic and fool-proof solution to the problem that we had identified. I tried to be empathetic toward the refugees' plight, but I did not know much about the issue, nor did I think it was relevant to me at all. However, we had the opportunity to meet with some stakeholders for our project, including a refugee student, who provided us with invaluable insight into the problems facing refugees in Malaysia. I was shocked to discover some behind-the-scenes injustice that was occurring in our own country. It was mind-boggling to know that a large number of refugees in Malaysia, especially children and adolescents, are unable to receive a proper education because of their refugee status.

These refugees were forced to flee their countries due to political instability and had no choice but to abandon their lives there and seek refuge in other, faraway countries. Imagine seeking refuge in a foreign land, only to be treated no better than illegal immigrants and criminals. Imagine trying to fight that injustice but eventually bowing to pressure and accepting everything, from fear of being thrown out of the only safe haven you know. That is reality for most refugees in the country. I can't imagine how tough it must be for the children to give up their schooling while still feeling the thirst to learn. Unfortunately, they are not given the same education privileges as Malaysian children. What is worse, they are treated unequally in our society.

The struggle facing refugees, especially children, around the world has made me realize that most of us take education for granted. Some of these kids are trying to get one tenth of the education that we get on a daily basis. Yet we sit here and complain about studying. In the current global refugee crisis, most countries are still treating refugees as somebody else's problem. I believe that countries that take in refugees should see the situation as an opportunity for the newcomers to integrate with the locals and contribute to our economic growth and society at large. We should provide refugee children with access to our education system instead of stopping these bright minds from realizing their potential due to lack of resources and basic educational rights. After doing much research and participating in discussions on the plight of refugees, I found that Malaysians are constantly worried about the influx of foreign workers in our country; they group refugees and asylum seekers with other types of immigrants.

I brought up this topic with some friends outside the ALY Camp, and they gave me blank stares, showing no interest whatsoever in the issue. They feel that the refugees' plight is fabricated, since foreign immigrants in the country are viewed negatively. That made me realize that it is our responsibility, especially for the young people of Malaysia, to help the refugees in our country by volunteering with organizations that offer help to these groups or joining leadership courses such as this one to learn how we can make a difference in society. The ALY Camp has truly inspired me to be more aware of current events and to help shape a better tomorrow. I am now more determined than ever to seek more knowledge and to find a solution to the refugee crisis one day. I wish to assist in any way that I can, especially in helping refugees find their voices and seize every opportunity to utilize their talents and capabilities, thus garnering the strength to build better lives for themselves.

Learning about refugees was a truly humbling experience, and I am grateful for the life I have now. There will always be someone out there going through a much worse time than I am. I know I should work hard to cherish whatever I have and give back to society. Many of us focus only on getting a well-paying job after graduation, losing sight of the simple act of helping others. Instead, we need to work together and set aside our differences to make the world a better place. I believe that education is key in solving most of the problems we face today. Issues such as racism, sex discrimination and even the plight of refugees are largely caused by ignorance and a lack of knowledge. Everyone should be more aware of current events, regardless of their backgrounds and positions in society. Everyone can contribute, no matter how little it may be, to nip these problems in the bud. Renowned education activists such as Malala Yousafzai and Michelle Obama are continuously striving to ensure that all members of society have equal rights to education. We, the youth, are leaders not only of tomorrow but of today. Hence, we should take charge of increasing the access to knowledge, making it available to all. I encourage the young generation to participate in humanitarian efforts led by nongovernmental organizations (NGOs) to help refugees. Becoming a leader means taking the first step toward making a difference, regardless of whether it is a small step, a leap or a jump. Everyone wants change, but no one brings it by themselves. Be the change you want to see in the world.

To sum up, I am an entirely different person after attending the ALY Camp. The old me was ignorant, fearful, anxious and confused. Now I am much more confident, focused, ambitious and energetic. In my daily life I am implementing the lessons I learned during my short stint at the ALY Camp, and it seems to be working well thus far. However, I am still open to any changes in my personality that might come about because of new life experiences. Life is a journey, and I am going to make mistakes. What is important is that I learn from those mistakes and continue to evolve in order to achieve my goals.

I look forward to helping others and imparting my knowledge, experiences and life lessons to those in need. I am glad to say that I have begun reaching out to people and helping them in their life journeys. Hopefully you too will be inspired to carve out your destiny and empower others to make a difference in the world. Dare to be naïve! Someday, love and peace will conquer all the troubles of the world. Together, we will make the world a better place! To quote *The Three Musketeers*, 'All for one, and one for all!'

| Chapter 7 |

Be Yourself and You Can Be Anything

Ong Qian Chern

● ● ●

'I am an introvert.' That was what I wrote last year. However, after participating twice in the ALY Camp, I no longer think of myself as a person who can't speak and remains quiet most of the time. I know now that I possess unique characteristics, and I can now say I am proud of them. Before the ALY Camp, I was not fond of being quiet, especially during group conversations. People tended to ignore me; they wouldn't even bother to look at me, at most they would just ask my name and age. Sometimes it bothered me, and I questioned why I was naturally more reserved. At this year's ALY Camp, however, I finally discovered that being quiet can actually work to my advantage.

On the first day of the ALY Camp, I was very excited to meet with the Harvard Teaching Fellows, the delegates and the Student Leaders. I introduced myself to everyone, and everything went smoothly at first. Then came the hard part: because of my quiet personality, I had a difficult time fitting in with the groups I found myself in, whether we were conducting group discussions or just normal conversations. I always wanted to say a few words or share my opinions, but I could barely say anything because everyone was so busy talking. They expressed their views, which basically encapsulated the things I wanted to say. The one time I got to speak was when they asked me, 'So what do you think of our ideas, do you like them?' and all I could answer was a straightforward 'yes' or 'no,' followed by a simple explanation. The only other chance I got to speak was when the Fellows asked for opinions during the workshops. Even then, many people were eager to share their views, and when I looked at the wave of hands, I figured I didn't stand a chance to speak. The only exception was if the Fellow specifically asked me to share my thoughts.

The first day was very challenging. I experienced the same thing over and over again in every workshop. I became really frustrated by my lack of ability to speak up. I thought that maybe I could share my frustration with my roommate, to get the weight off my chest, but he was busy preparing for his upcoming international Biology Olympiad as well as completing other tasks for the workshops. We talked a little, but seeing that he was preoccupied with his preparations, I didn't share my frustration with him. With no one to talk to, I kept everything inside. I decided to sleep, hoping that the next day would be better and that I would muster the courage to change.

When I woke up the next day, I headed to the bathroom and looked at my reflection in the mirror. All I saw was a dejected boy looking back at me. I told myself not to give up just because of a little hardship. I reminded myself of the challenges that the Fellows had shared yesterday in their stories and gave myself a pep talk, telling myself not to give up. Instead, I should step up to the plate and accept the challenge to improve.

I had a rough start that day, but instead of throwing in the towel again, I decided to go and talk to some other people who were like me. I started to engage in conversations with them, and that was when I began to feel that I was making progress. I finally made some new friends, and although I still faced the same problem during group discussions, I tried to contribute whenever possible. Every little step counts!

On the second day, Ms. Lee asked to come up with a solution to the refugee crisis in Malaysia. Later that evening, she conducted an extra class to clarify the purpose of the design challenge and to describe how to apply it accurately. After her explanation, a lot of people realized that their ideas were not really relevant to the refugee project—in fact, what everyone had done so far was basically wrong. Most of the groups started to feel conflicted, including mine. With all the disagreements, the situation became pretty bad. When I was about to leave, I noticed that one of my friends looked sad. He was upset that his teammates were not being cooperative during discussions and that he was always the one who ended up doing the work. He was ready to give up, but I advised him to carry on. At that moment, I realized that I am a good listener. People can come to me and share their pent-up anger and frustration. For once, I felt happy about my introvert self, which attracts others to confide in me. I was starting to learn to appreciate and embrace my personality. Everyone is different and unique in their own way.

The following days gave me more opportunities to learn and gain insights into the topics of discussion. Ms. Lee's case analysis framework during her 'Personal Leadership' workshop was very helpful. It helped us to see things in a bigger picture and encouraged analytical thinking. In Mr. Tarnowski's workshop, 'Cross-Cultural Competencies,' I discovered the importance of tolerance for ambiguity. When different cultures meet, it is easy for us to judge, but it is important to take the initiative to get to know the other culture better. We have to be patient and tolerant enough to understand a certain culture in order for us to promote engagement with others and embrace diversity.

Meanwhile, Mr. Kim's workshop on developing your personal brand struck a chord with me. The stories that he told us about his hardships in life as well as the difficulties faced by famous people throughout history motivated me to be strong in times of trial. I shouldn't cry in a corner and expect my problems to go away by themselves. Instead I should be optimistic and embrace a positive outlook toward life. These key takeaways helped me to re-evaluate my strengths and weaknesses and to identify ways to improve myself. By using the case-analysis framework, I reflected on why am I such a quiet person and the factors that have contributed to my character. Tolerance for ambiguity taught me to be more open in accepting others, especially the new people I meet. We tend to judge others by their appearances, but really we should take the time to know more about them, asking questions to demonstrate interest in their backgrounds and personalities. We should also be more empathetic and help others, as they may be in a tough situation and need someone to talk to.

Each workshop taught us different things, but together they made us realize that we should try to know more about ourselves through reflection. Instead of calling it a one-week intensive leadership course, I prefer calling it a one-week intensive self-reflection program. During each workshop, the Fellows would ask us the same question regardless of the issues at hand: 'What do you think?' Sometimes they would give us a statement, such as 'I want you to think about the past few moments and how they affected you.' They wanted us to think continuously about the reasons behind every problem and about what we would do if we were in a position to manage the issue. This encouraged us to find our true selves. Self-reflection does not require physical activity, but it can still be exhausting! Nevertheless, it was worth it, as I now understand the importance of putting ourselves in other people's shoes in order to come up with solutions for the problems at hand. Doing so encourages us to identify our strengths and weaknesses so that we can better face future challenges.

Despite these positive experiences, my joy was short-lived. While we were preparing our presentation for the refugee project, my teammates did not assign me any tasks for the PowerPoint slides. I had a feeling that it was because of my quiet personality. As a result, I sat quietly in one corner, doing nothing while the rest of them were busy with the preparations. I offered to help, but they did not need my assistance. I retired early, feeling frustrated and cowardly for not speaking up. At the dorm, I saw my Student Leader relaxing in his room and decided to confide in him. He told me that the ALY Camp was designed to enable people from different backgrounds to learn how to communicate and socialize with new friends. He encouraged me to initiate conversations more often. I felt that it was unfair that none of my teammates had given me the opportunity to speak or contribute to the group's preparation. But I was a different person when I talked to the Student Leader. I became talkative, venting my frustration and sharing my thoughts with him. The Student Leader was shocked to see me speaking eloquently without any inhibitions. Then I realized that being quiet can also lead to being misunderstood. The Student Leader suggested that I learn to express my feelings more often and to give others the chance to know me better. I was grateful to him for giving me a shoulder to cry on. There and then, I decided to redeem myself and reach out to others to make more connections.

The next day, I didn't want to make any drastic changes. I listened attentively to the other delegates' stories and decided to share my thoughts as well. It was the first time that I had opened up to the rest of them. As I spoke, I realized the things that I should do if I wish to carve a better path for my future. I need to change and grow as a person to create my own destiny. I also realized that I was not the only one who thought that way—all of us discovered the same need to work hard at achieving our life goals.

At the graduation dinner, I wanted to ask Mr. Kim if I should contribute a chapter on my ALY Camp experience for the upcoming book. I had trouble speaking at first, but Mr. Kim encouraged me, which gave me the confidence to change and contribute to the community at large. Although I was relieved that the ALY Camp was over, I knew that in the future I need to step out of my comfort zone if I want to accomplish great things in life. Yes, I might fail, but the most important thing is that I learn from my failure and pick myself up. The world is full of opportunities, but still I must seize every opportunity that comes or it may pass me by. The ALY Camp taught me all these things, and no words can describe how glad I am for attending it.

Although the ALY Camp has now ended, that doesn't mean I can crawl back to my comfort zone and shut myself off from society. Instead it marks a new beginning. From now on, I am committed to being more honest and brave in reaching out to people and expressing myself clearly and eloquently. I have realized that the ability to communicate well is an essential skill in life. I need to challenge myself and be more confident if I want to go far. With that said, I am still quiet, and I have begun to see my quietness as a strength. It allows me to be a good listener and helps me to connect to the world. I want readers out there to appreciate who they really are. Be yourself and build your own personal brand. By cultivating self-acceptance, we will be much happier and more confident in going through life's incredible journey.

| Chapter 8 |
An Unexpected Journey

Loh Lynn Way

● ● ●

When my parents encouraged me to attend the ALY Camp, I told them that I would think about it, which in teenager language means 'No thanks.' I consider myself to be someone who gets bored easily. The idea of doing the same thing for a long period of time terrifies me. So I was not looking forward to a six-day youth camp.

A few weeks prior to the ALY Camp, a few of the Harvard Teaching Fellows and committee members held a small talk to introduce the ALY Camp. Somehow, my parents persuaded me to go, and on the same night they signed me up. I reluctantly filled in the registration form. Even though my parents tried to talk me into it and explained the ALY Camp's benefits, I still went home with doubts in my head and a frown on my face. Little did I know at the time that the things I learned at the ALY Camp would stick with me for a long time.

The first day started with a plenary session, conducted by Mr.

Kim, about developing a personal brand and a successful career path. He divided us into a few groups, and we were told to pair up and ask our partner a series of questions. That activity made me feel more comfortable with the other delegates, and also made me question my identity and goals in life. As homework, we had to draw a life diagram and write down our key moments in life, which made me reflect on my life and think about my strengths and weaknesses. Life is tough, and success does not come easily. I now realized that to achieve success, everyone endures difficult moments. However, we should see this as a challenge and take the opportunity to leverage on our strengths to overcome our weaknesses, maintaining a positive mindset. The session taught me to channel my knowledge, skills and passion for the benefit of the community at large.

Mr. Kim also gave us a sneak peek into his life, in which he had to work at many different jobs before finding his calling. It made me think that everything comes with a cost. If we want to succeed, we have to work hard. If we fail, we should learn from the experience and pick ourselves up again. Life is full of ups and downs. We should never give up but continue fighting and be patient in facing challenges. Only then will we reap the fruits of our labor. History has shown that many great leaders faced failures, but the hardships only made them stronger. These are the role models that we should look up to as we power through adversity. For example, Abraham Lincoln encountered many failures. In his early life, he tried starting a few businesses, but they never materialized. He later ran for Congress, Senate and Vice President, but lost each time. Even though he did not succeed in his first few tries, he kept persevering and was finally elected as President of the Unites States in 1860. He managed to achieve his goals because he never stopped trying. Even today, he remains a role model and an inspiration to many people around the world.

The plenary session inspired me to plan out my future goals and what I need to do to achieve them. For one of our last homework assignments, we were required to design epitaphs for our own tombstones. It might sound a bit odd, but while working on the activity I realized that I had never thought before about the legacy I will leave behind after my time on earth is over. Of course, my initial thought was that I wanted to leave behind a legacy of good impressions. I knew, though, that my epitaph had to be something more specific and significant. One of the core things that I learned from the ALY Camp is that you have to go the extra mile and reach for the farthest thing out there. I had never understood before that every little action every day can impact the future. After much thought, I decided that I wanted to be a creator. Although I will never know if this epitaph will really be mine, I am determined to make something and leave a mark on this world. It could be through a piece of art, writing or anything that allows me to express myself. I know I will have to work hard to realize my goal, but I am confident that the advice and knowledge I gained from the ALY Camp will fuel my ambition.

During Ms. Lee's plenary session, we were required to develop a solution for the refugee issue. We were separated into groups, and I was glad to have easy-going teammates to work with who were willing to spend hours together, even till the wee hours of the night, to find the perfect solution. It took us four days to complete the presentation, using different techniques taught by Ms. Lee, one of which was 'Design Thinking.' This technique required us to develop ideas or solutions based on a certain scenario. Our teamwork skills were really tested through this experience, as we had to work together in a short amount of time—a minute or so—to complete the task. Ms. Lee would ask a question regarding refugees, such as 'What do you think goes through a refugee's mind throughout the day?' and we had to write as many answers as possible on sticky notes and place them on a piece of paper on the wall. After the first round, we had a clearer idea on what to expect in the next round. The problem statement that my group came up with was 'Refugee children lack education due to the language barrier,' and we proposed 'Recruiting refugees to educate their youth' as the solution. We managed to come up with the solution thanks to the representatives from the United Nations High Commission for Refugees (UNHCR) and Cyber Care, who helped us with the research and group discussions. The activity really opened my eyes to the current refugee situation in Malaysia. I became more aware of how often refugees are misunderstood and mistreated. Everyone in the group not only managed to bond through this experience but also learned the values of working as a team and the real meaning behind the expression 'Many hands make lighter work.'

I was also impressed with Mr. Kim's 'Negotiation Leadership' workshop. I learned so many things in it that I had never thought about prior to joining the ALY Camp. The main takeaway from the workshop was that trust is a very important factor, in starting a business or even in doing something as simple as trading things with a friend. To test this theory out, we were paired up and given a scenario: one of us was the buyer, and the other was the seller. The task was to sell or buy an object at a price that would give us the most profit. The concepts of 'Best Alternatives to a Negotiated Agreement' (BATNA) and 'Zone of Possible Agreement' (ZOPA) were used to improve our negotiation skills. BATNAs mean that both parties determine the outcome if they cannot come to an agreement, while ZOPAs refer to a price between two figures that will benefit both parties. By identifying our BATNAs and ZOPAs, we were able to distinguish a suitable price as well as some alternatives to selling or buying.

I did not consider myself a good negotiator, but the workshop helped me to think of different ways and strategies to negotiate in business. On the last day, we were divided into groups of four. Each of us represented a different country and pretended that we were the CEOs of large oil companies. The goal was to earn as much money as you could by setting the price of your oil either on the high or low end of the price range. Of course, the profits depended on the choices made by the other three companies as well. The activity lasted ten rounds, and we learned that we all had to cooperate so that none of us would lose money. In order to gain the largest amount of money, a person might set his or her price on the low end while everyone else set their prices on the high end. For the first few rounds, we weren't given the opportunity to discuss or negotiate, so it all relied on luck. If the group was fortunate enough, everyone would benefit. Unfortunately, my group was not so successful; some of us profited, while others had losses. Then there was a round in which we were given the chance to converse with each other, and our final decision was for everyone to set their price on the high end so that everyone could benefit a little. Out of nowhere, however, someone in our group decided to set their price on the low end, causing the rest of us to lose money while they gained profits. After that unexpected experience, we had a hard time trusting each other in the next few rounds. At the end of the experiment, Mr. Kim explained that there was a way that would allow all of us to obtain a stable profit: if we all worked together and trusted each other. But since some decided to boycott the group's decision for their own benefit, trust was not an option in the following rounds. That taught me the importance of teamwork and of gaining everyone's trust if we want to live in harmony with everyone, including our rivals. Although it might seem hard, it will ultimately benefit all parties.

I also attended the 'Cross-Cultural Competencies' workshop conducted by Mr. Tarnowski. The workshop was fascinating. Not only did I learn the importance of cooperating with people of different cultures, I also got to experience it myself. One activity that really stood out during the ALY Camp and has stuck with me even now was an exercise in which Mr. Tarnowski divided the class into two groups, one representing the Hokies and the other representing the Heelotians. The Hokies and Heelotians come from places with completely different cultures. Each group was given a list of questions about the other team. Our goal was to discover how to communicate with people from the other culture and get our questions answered. I was one of the Hokies, and even though I did not represent my group to communicate with the Heelots, I could still tell how hard it was to engage with them or even start a conversation. It took us many tries before we actually got somewhere, and by the time we had got the hang of it, we had already run out of time. This really made me reflect on the way we treat people of different races and cultures in Malaysia. Our country is known for its diversity and the fact that everyone lives in harmony despite our differences. Of course, it may not apply to every single person in Malaysia, but a majority of us find it easy to communicate with one another and feel comfortable with people of different races.

Besides that, Mr. Tarnowski, taught us about Hofstede's Cultural Dimension, which revolves around cultural differences and how they affect the workplace. We studied the four dimensions: 'Power Distance,' 'Individualism vs. Collectivism,' 'Uncertainty Avoidance' and 'Masculinity vs. Femininity.' The concepts describe the effects of a society's culture on the values of its members. We also worked on various case studies about how people from different cultures can get along in the workplace. These case studies taught me that we must be rational in decision making and ensure that everyone has a say, regardless of the nature of their opinions. Everyone has their own way of getting things done, and if someone does something differently it does not necessarily mean that they are inefficient. Probably it simply means that that is how things are done in their culture.

All work and no play makes Jack a dull boy. In the evenings, we participated in activities that enabled us to relax and bond with our fellow delegates and Teaching Fellows. These activities included ice skating, a captain ball tournament and zumba. It was great to sweat it out and work as a team with the other delegates.

I will always remember one particular activity called the 'Dialogue in the Dark,' which showed us how it feels to live in the dark. We were separated into groups and entered a dark room together. We were not given any tools to help us see apart from a white cane. A visually impaired person assisted us in navigating through the room. It amazed me that he was able to do almost everything a person with normal vision can. He told us about his hobbies, and we learned about his hometown. I have to admit, it was quite hard for me to walk around without the fear of getting lost or falling over. We had to use our other senses to find our way through the place. After that short twenty minutes in the dark, I realized how lucky I was to have perfect eyesight and learned to not take anything, especially my five senses, for granted.

On the last day, we participated in a community service project called 'Random Acts of Kindness,' held at the Sunway Pyramid Shopping Mall. In the project, we gave out free hugs, compliments and little notes with nice messages to shoppers. We had to deal with rejection a couple of times, but when people responded positively, it made us happy and motivated us to keep moving on and putting a smile on someone's face. Now I always remind myself to spread good will wherever I go, and also to encourage others to do the same. You never know how much simple gestures, such as saying 'Thank you!' or smiling, can brighten up someone's day.

The last activity at the ALY Camp required us to write and deliver a speech on a topic we feel passionate about. Mr. Tarnowski offered us tips and rules in delivering a good speech. He showed us videos of various role models and world leaders presenting iconic speeches to help us understand the skills involved. I discovered a concept called Aristotle's Persuasion Framework that helped me make a good speech. According to the framework, a good speech must include Logos, Pathos and Ethos, which translate to logic/reason, emotions/values and credibility/trust. After this task I now understand that when speaking in public I must include a story of self, a story of now and a story of us. This helps to hold the audience's attention by encouraging them to relate to the current situation and by persuading them to lend a helping hand to overcome a certain issue.

Even though I did not have much time to prepare the speech, I still managed to write a decent one, thanks to Mr. Tarnowski and my groupmates' help. One person from each group was chosen to present his or her speech in front of everyone. Three people were also given the chance to present their speeches at the graduation dinner. Although I was not chosen to deliver my speech, I was still glad that I had the opportunity to present my speech in front of my groupmates and to learn about my strengths and weaknesses. Thanks to this experience, I realized that in a world where everyone strives to be the one in the spotlight, there will always be a need for people to help and support the leaders. Many people out there have the talent to deliver amazing speeches. They can make dull sentences sound interesting. However, there are other people out there who write incredible content but need help to improve their speaking skills. With the help of my groupmates, we learned that we all have different personalities, and through the feedback we received from each other, we managed to discover our weaknesses. Most importantly, we all utilized our strengths to help each other grow and improve.

In conclusion, the six days spent at the ALY Camp really impacted my life for the better. I met many people that I can call friends to this day, learned new skills and, most importantly, got to know myself a lot better. At the ALY Camp, I discovered that there is nothing wrong with looking into the past and reflecting on your mistakes; that is how you grow as an individual, by failing and turning it into something that motivates you to succeed in the future. I also learned that stepping out of your comfort zone is really important when it comes to acquiring new skills and knowledge. There were many times when I felt shy about answering a question or even giving my opinion, but I learned to overcome the fear because I realized that many opportunities come only once. I hope to take the lessons that I have learned to further improve myself and to make a positive impact on other people's lives. I wish to thank the ALY Camp organizers for making my experience an enjoyable and unforgettable one. I will definitely use the insights and lessons I learned from the ALY Camp to inspire others.

Part 2

:

Global Leadership Trek

| Chapter 9 |

Forging My Own Path to Success

Mengheng Lim

● ● ●

"Better to see something once than to hear about it a thousand times."
— Asian proverb

New York City

From Excitement to Confusion

After surviving a 25-hour-plus flight, the plane finally touched down on American soil, and I couldn't wait to get out of the aircraft and explore 'the land of the free.' I couldn't contain my excitement. 'I am finally here!' The two-week adventure known as the Global Leadership Trek (GLT) offered me a golden opportunity to visit Ivy League universities and renowned organizations in the U.S. and to explore what it takes to be one of the next generation of leaders.

However, my heart quickly shifted from excitement to confusion upon entering the JFK Airport terminal. I expected it to be in one of the busiest and most modern airports in the world, but it turned out to be an outdated airport. I started to wonder what I should expect after leaving the airport. Would the buildings in the city look old too? While waiting for the other Trekkers to arrive, I decided to hop on the internal transfer train to check out the other six terminals, to see if there were any differences between them and the terminal I had just exited. There was not much difference.

A few minutes after we left the airport, I was pleased to see that the roads were well-built and designed to accommodate a high number of vehicles. Still, I couldn't see any high-rise structures yet—though I might have missed the view because I fell asleep during the ride.

The night was too short. My body had not had enough time to recover from tiredness, but it was time to explore New York City. All the Trekkers convened in the hostel lobby and listened to Mr. John Lim, our Trek leader, as he urged us to head out. I did not see any signs, so I just followed my fellow Trekkers, who were entering the entrance to an underground tunnel. I wondered what this place was and later learned that it was the subway station. The wind was blowing inside the station, but my body temperature increased dramatically. It was weird, like being in the desert. Besides its aging and hot condition, the station was huge and made me wonder how engineers in the last century could have built such a big underground station. When we left the subway, we were in downtown Manhattan. I was mesmerized by the large number of high-rise buildings, especially the architectural beauty of the Rockefeller Center.

There is a Cambodian proverb which says, 'Never forget about the root.' The proverb refers to the fact that the Cambodian people had to endure immense suffering during the four-year reign of the Khmer Rouge. They had to start all over again after the civil war ended, followed by another decade of instability. I grew up in a small town in the countryside called Neak Leoung, where there is nothing much besides rice fields and fishing places along the Mekong River. It is famous only because the east and the west parts of the town are divided by the river. Although the national road network has connected the capital city of Phnom Penh to Ho Chi Minh City through Neak Leoung for many years, all vehicles used to have to stop at this area while waiting for the ferry to cross the river. The waiting time could be more than ten hours during national holiday, such as the Khmer New Year. The people wished for a bridge to connect the two parts of the town. Finally, last year, twenty years after I was born, the bridge was built and soon became the symbol of the town. It has been years since things started to develop throughout Cambodia, especially concrete buildings and infrastructure. However, I feel that the current development is not sufficient and not up to par with what the Cambodian people were accustomed to before the civil war. A lesson from Mr. Vann Molyvann, a well-known 1950s Cambodian architect, also known as 'the man who built Cambodia,' was that we still need more buildings, infrastructure and sustainable development, and especially more well-planned cities. For example, it should not have taken such a long time to build a bridge connecting the two parts of Neak Leoung.

The GLT offered me a great opportunity to come to the U.S. and observe developments in that part of the world, giving me a new perspective on what my country could do to develop its cities in the field of engineering. I was very eager to learn and gain more knowledge from the Trek, as it tied into my passion for social entrepreneurship. I am studying engineering, and I hope to contribute to Cambodia in this area. I would like to make a difference and become a leader of tomorrow. I believed that the Trek would let me see things from a different perspective and improve my learning skills.

The Open Society Foundations: How People View and React to World Issues

We received a warm welcome by the Open Society Foundations (OSF), a non-profit organization founded by Mr. George Soros, a successful business magnate who has a passion for helping people in various societies across the world. It was my first time visiting such a renowned organization abroad. The OSF is situated in a large building with a conducive work environment, which looks very different from the offices in Cambodia. On our visit, I learned that all of us has the responsibiltiy to change the world and make it a better place by solving issues related to education, health, human rights and justice.

During our visit, we engaged in a fascinating sharing session that enabled us to learn more about each other. An OSF staff explained that she was born in Vietnam and migrated to Cambodia during the Khmer Rouge regime before coming to the U.S. During that period, very few people could escape the military and go to the United Nations camp on the Thai-Cambodian border before departing to another country. The hardships she endured then led her to join the OSF and help other people who are in need.

My experience at the OSF prompted me to think that more business people in Cambodia should step up to the plate and emulate Mr. Soros by giving back to society and paving the way for sustainable and equitable prosperity in the country. For example, Dr. Mengly J. Quach left Cambodia during the Khmer Rouge reign and ultimately obtained his education in the U.S. After almost thirty years abroad, he returned to Cambodia and promoted sustainable development in the country through social entrepreneurship. He established the Mengly J. Quach Education, which focuses on education, health and social and community development. People like Dr. Quach have inspired me to start a business venture to develop and implement innovative solutions to social and environmental problems. I believe that this is an effective way to improve the standard of living in developing countries like Cambodia.

The story is very similar for many Cambodian people, including my parents, who migrated to neighboring countries during the civil war. This terrifying experience will be forever etched in the minds of our people, especially the elderly. To the best of my knowledge, there are more than thirty thousand Cambodian Americans, the majority of whom were born in Cambodia. This is a significant number for a nation that has a total population of fifteen million. The Cambodians abroad live in a better condition, with a higher standard of education, than most of the Khmer people in Cambodia. Although they live overseas, they are committed to the development of their country of birth. However, many of them focus on political issues in Cambodia, which is unfortunate. I feel that they should focus on ways to contribute to the improvement of living standards, like Dr. Quach.

Meeting with April Bank: Another Perspective on Leadership

After a long day in the hot weather, our dinner at an Italian restaurant was a welcome escape. There were almost fifty options available on the menu, but I knew only one Italian dish that I loved to eat—spaghetti carbonara. After a few minutes, a woman walked in and talked to the waiter; her face looked puzzled, as if she were looking for a group of people. Suddenly my fellow Trekker, Felicia saw her and signaled for her to come to our table. The woman was Ms. April Bank, a Harvard graduate and a PhD candidate with experiences in teaching leadership programs in different regions.

It was a great opportunity for all of us to learn life lessons. After everyone had introduced themselves, we continued our discussion. I was surprised when Ms. Bank suddenly stopped talking in the middle of the discussion. We were confused and kept staring at each other. Ms. Bank then explained to us that she had stopped talking because she wanted to see the dynamic flow of the conversation and was waiting for everyone to come up with their own ideas for the discussion. Ms. Bank also taught us about ways to improve our leadership skills and how to work in a team. For example, everyone needs to be proactive and grab any chance that we have to voice our opinion. Ms. Bank shared with us the challenges that she has faced as a woman in a leadership role; she suggested being neutral and stepping back a bit to reflect before taking action, when going through a crisis. Her stories showed that gender inequality in leadership is still present and that everyone, women and men, including me, should work together to solve this issue by providing more opportunities to women. Then

Felicia shared her own leadership challenges and how she overcame them. She added that women should turn challenges into opportunities and prove men wrong.

At the end of the discussion, I had come to believe that all present and future leaders should value women's roles in society, especially in developing countries. This reminded me of the misconception in Cambodia that there are things that men can do and women can't. Society's perception has changed over time, but a majority of Cambodian people in less developed areas still follow this concept and do not allow women to work outside their hometowns. I have two sisters, and I can see that they could accomplish anything that a man could do, sometimes even better than a man. As I aim to become a contributing member of society, I believe that women can do whatever they want, and, hopefully, I will be able to help empower women to participate fully in all sectors for the betterment of the community.

Columbia University: Equal Opportunities for High-Quality Education

Coming to the U.S. is a dream for many people, but not everyone can do so. Many students also harbor the desire to further their studies in the U.S. Hence, I was really grateful to be given the opportunity to participate in the GLT. I am also thankful that my parents supported my ambition to join the Trek and to explore educational opportunities in the States.

Columbia University was the first institute of higher learning that we visited. It was one of many universities I had wanted to visit before going on the Trek. After entering the university grounds, I thought we would explore the beautiful surroundings, which included two museums. However, we had to rush to the university information session. The university building was beautiful and exquisite. Later we went on a campus tour. The campus was big and stunning compared to my university back home. I was impressed by the buildings' unique architectural designs, which differ each from another. Most of the buildings reflected western architectural styles, which I had never seen before.

Initially, I thought it would be difficult to enter a highly ranked university like Columbia, but our meeting with the admissions officer quelled my reservations. I strongly believe that everyone has an equal opportunity to gain access to high-quality education. Everyone should stop dreaming, wake up and seize the resources out there to realize their dreams.

Washington, D.C.

First Impression: A Well-Designed City

Upon our arrival in Washington, D.C., I was surprised by the city's layout, cleanliness and population. The U.S. capital is more laid-back than New York City. Public transportation in the city, such as the Rail Rapid Transit system and buses, made it convenient for everyone to move around. I had a pleasant experience leading my fellow Trekkers when we commuted from one place to another during our five-day stay. Moreover, the subway stations displayed modern architecture, built in a semi-cylindrical shape without any column support in the middle. The famous Cambodian architect, Mr. Molyvann, once said that each building must be unique and original. D.C. was a beautiful city and clearly reflected that ethos. Additionally, D.C. had so many parks and open spaces that it did not surprise me to see the people there leading a city lifestyle while still enjoying leisure pursuits such as running and cycling.

Museums, the United States and the Outside World

Even though Washington, D.C. is a small city, it is the U.S.'s historical and political hub. It is a city of museums, and one of my favorites was the Newseum, which demonstrates the evolution of print and electronic communication from the U.S.'s earliest days until today. It showcases not only U.S.-related events but also fascinating stories between the U.S. and other nations. My two favorite stories were the U.S.-Vietnam war and the 9/11 terrorist attacks in 2001. While I was excited to learn more about the U.S.-Vietnam war, I was shocked to learn the number of U.S. military fatalities in the war, which was a lot higher than those of other wars, including the World Wars.

Unfortunately, the Newseum did not showcase news stories that were related to Cambodia during the U.S.-Vietnam war, though many Cambodians believe that Cambodia was somehow involved in the war. The museum also displayed tools, clothing and equipment used during the war. Seeing all of the items on display, I could imagine how tough it was for people living in war-torn countries. Most Cambodians have experienced difficult living conditions since the 1970s, especially the older generation, who always told us stories about how they survived the civil war and continued living without hope. These stories serve as a constant reminder of how lucky we are to have been born after the war.

International Leadership Foundation: Building Bridges

Next on our program was a visit to the International Leadership Foundation (ILF), a non-profit organization that promotes the civic awareness, public service and economic prosperity of the Asian Pacific American community. We met with Ms. Sookyung, the only full-time employee at the ILF. She shared with us the organization's goals and explained that the Foundation's mission is to build bridges among young leaders in the U.S., Asia and the Pacific Rim countries through a network of business and community leaders. This grabbed my attention, as it reminded me of a rift between Cambodia and Thailand over the ownership of the Preah Vihear Temple, a UNESCO World Heritage Site. The International Court of Justice in The Hague ruled in favor of Cambodia, but the education systems in both countries offer different information with regard to the issue, intensifying the disagreement. After discovering what the ILF is all about, I decided that we should find ways to improve the relationship between Cambodia and Thailand, including facilitating effective discussions to encourage dialogue between the two countries. During our meeting with the ILF, I got a better understanding of its organizational structure, which is divided into two branches. The first one is the executive branch, responsible for executing projects within and outside the U.S. The other branch consists of the management board, in which decisions are made by donors and prominent professionals. The meeting enabled me to learn about running an organization and effective ways of dividing tasks and responsibilities for different teams.

Every organization faces various challenges, including working with people from culturally diverse backgrounds. People have different values and characteristics, and it is crucial to adapt to the situation when dealing with cross-cultural issues at the workplace. To me, this as an advantage, as we can see things from different perspectives and thus expand our mindset.

I was surprised when Ms. Sookyung mentioned that technology was a challenge for her, though information technology is an effective tool in her work. Additionally, she briefed us on how to get support from donors: it is important to focus on more than just presenting the best pitch; we also need to partner with organizations with similar missions so that they can share the grants for their project. The meeting reminded me of my business class during my freshman year at university, which taught me that we can persuade successful business people to fund a start-up if we manage to present a convincing pitch. Although I have not worked for any organizations yet, my past experience of running a social entrepreneurship club has led me to believe that if I learn how an organization works, I will be able to achieve greater results. I will definitely apply what I learned at the ILF in my future endeavors. Moreover, the experience gave me invaluable insights into construction management, a field that I am interested in pursuing in the future. Running an organization effectively is an important factor in carrying out successful construction projects.

Before we left, Ms. Sookyung gave us inspiring advice: 'Don't limit yourself.' This phrase made me think about opportunities in the past in which I missed out due to lack of confidence. For example, I never believed that I could come to an Ivy League university. Now that I have visited the U.S., my future goal is to pursue my higher education there. Ms. Sookyung's advice has spurred me to work harder and believe in myself. She gave me the confidence to face my fears and overcome roadblocks in order to achieve my goals. It is up to me to take up challenges and turn them into opportunities. I now realize that I need to take action and be more active to reach my goals.

At the same time, I need to be realistic and understand that things may not always work out as expected. For now, I will start applying for a job to gain more experience in the area of construction management, while waiting for admission into a U.S. university. Besides occupying my time efficiently, I believe that such a job will give me the added advantage in gaining entrance to a reputable university.

Boston

A High-Ranking Educational Hub

When I first arrived in Boston, I was excited to visit my dream universities, the Massachusetts Institute of Technology (MIT) and Harvard University. Education is an integral part of Boston's brand, and the city is a hub of international students from all over the world.

During the Trek, we spent time with a Harvard professor who shared with us his background and working life at the Ivy League university. Even though the professor was in the medical field, he tried to relate his story to other areas of interest, including business and engineering. Now I am more motivated than ever to work hard to achieve my goal.

Learning from Other People's Experiences

I was happy to meet Ms. Erin Linn, the founder of Integrated Heritage Project, a non-profit organization that focuses on the conservation of cultural heritage in developing countries. I was especially excited about the meeting in which I discovered that she had chosen Cambodia for her pilot project. I support her technique to help Cambodian society, which involves bringing international experts to work in Cambodia. This method allows the international experts to impart their knowledge and skills to the Cambodians while learning about the local culture as well. I appreciate Ms. Linn's hard work and commitment in helping developing countries to gain access to education and growth. Later, I found out that the Kerdomnel Khmer Foundation for the Preservation and Conservation of Cambodia Culture and Heritage, which was founded by my instructor at Zaman University, shared the same mission as Ms. Linn's organization, so I suggested that she meet with him and said I would be more than happy to help arrange the meeting.

Experience is the best teacher. Observing other people's experiences gives us a foundation to understand problems that we may face in the future and enables us to acquire an edge by learning from other people who have already gone down the route we are traveling. Meeting these people and listening to their stories have inspired me to be more proactive, and I will definitely put the knowledge I gained during the Trek into action once I return to Cambodia.

Next Step Forward

The GLT taught me that when we make a decision, we need to ensure that we commit to it and follow through on it to realize our dreams. As mentioned earlier, I have always wanted to pursue my graduate studies in the U.S. The Trek allowed me to meet with successful professionals in their respective fields. This enabled me to attain invaluable knowledge and insights based on my observations and interactions, which has influenced my decision making process.

For example, Mr. John Lee, one of the GLT's Teaching Fellows, shared his experience of applying to universities. He advised me to include universities that have a higher acceptance rate rather than just focusing on prestigious schools that have strict requirements for admission. As a result, I have added universities such as George Washington University to my list. He also explained the importance of having a competitive edge in order to stand out from the crowd, and he said that drafting an exceptional university admission essay is a way to get noticed among thousands of applicants. He gave me advice and tips on how to write an unforgettable essay. His experience in recruiting people taught me the best way to craft a compelling resume to prepare myself for the working world.

I now realize that the world is a global village. Sometimes we forget that we are connected to other countries in countless ways, as we are too caught up in domestic affairs. As global citizens, however, we should see ourselves as part of the world community. All of us are responsible for problems that affect the world community, such as poverty and inequalities. We need innovative leaders to drive positive social change, promote inclusive growth and put the world on a more sustainable path. I aspire to be part of the future generation of leaders, and, as I highlighted earlier, I wish to enter the field of construction management. Hopefully, one day, I will be able to contribute to the development and progress of my country.

The GLT was an eye-opening experience and gave me an extraordinary opportunity to gain firsthand exposure to a different culture and to the challenges facing the international community. I am pleased to have been part of this memorable two-week journey, exploring the vibrant cities of New York City, Washington, D.C. and Boston with my fellow Trekkers, who shared a common passion to learn about leadership development and empowerment. The Trek was designed to give us an experiential education beyond the classroom, to nurture our intellectual curiosity and to enhance our decision making skills, as we seek effective ways to turn our aspirations into reality.

I have gained so much from the Trek, and it would be a waste not to put what I have learned into practice. Practice forms habits, and I am confident that soon I will be one step closer to making my dreams come true.

| Chapter 10 |

A Journey to Discovery

Maika Tsuchiya

● ● ●

Takeoff

'Our flight time to JFK airport is expected to be thirteen hours. We hope you will enjoy your flight with us. Thank you.'

I was extremely excited to know that I would be able to enjoy the throbbing of the jet engines and the air turbulence for over half a day. It was my first time traveling alone for over ten days, but I felt no fear as I looked forward to Trekking in the U.S., where I plan to further my studies as an undergraduate student.

Taking a Step Forward

As we flew through the bumpy air, I recalled my last trip to the U.S. When I was fifteen years old, my mother and I went on a group tour to New York City, Philadelphia, Boston and Washington, D.C.

While it was enjoyable to visit a number of famous tourist attractions, there was less opportunity to experience American customs and the real lives of Americans, as we had only six days and stayed in hotels.

Whenever I visit a foreign country, I try to discover differences between the country and Japan. For instance, when I went to Turkey two years ago, I visited some archaeological sites, mosques and bazaars. The exotic and beautiful sites evoked gasps of admiration from me. On the other hand, I saw some problems there. Children were selling bottles of water and yo-yos to foreign tourists around the mosque instead of going to school. Others were shining men's shoes at the bazaar. At the main entrance of the bazaar, a mother was sitting on the ground, holding her motionless baby in front of a small paper box with a few coins inside. Most of them were refugees. By paying attention to these aspects of Turkish life, I was able to learn about some of the problems in Turkish society, which sparked my interest in news relevant to European and Middle Eastern countries, including Turkey.

My mother often takes me with her to travel around the world. I have visited over twenty countries, from Asia to Europe, since I was eight years old. When I tell this fact to other people, some ask me if my parents work for a famous international organization or if I have ever lived in foreign countries. Then I explain to them that my parents manage local businesses and that I am an ordinary high school student, born and raised in Japan. I am graduating from a private school located in a suburban area in Chiba Prefecture. My school does not provide any special courses for students who wish to study abroad. However, my travels have given me the opportunity to discover social issues and cutting-edge technologies around the world.

This has led me to aspire to learn about advanced science in the U.S. and to become a biologist who works in the international community.

In order to get one step closer to my goal, I started studying English intensively and joined a lot of extracurricular activities to broaden my perspective, so that I would be able to communicate with students from various backgrounds. Additionally, I enrolled in some science programs held at a university to gain a better understanding of science. Yet I could not take part in the activities I was most interested in because there were no English-speaking partners available. Whenever I joined extramural academic programs, I would meet a lot of returnee students with multicultural backgrounds who had gone to international schools or other elite schools in Japan. While it was great for me to study with bright students, it sometimes intimidated me, as they were all perfect candidates for admission to U.S. universities. I asked myself, 'Do I deserve to study with these wonderful students?' As I accumulated experience in working with students from various backgrounds, I began to see myself as a unique student, but they were still far better at communicating with a diverse group of people, which is a necessary skill in building networks in an ethnically and culturally diverse country. My desire to improve this skill led me to join the GLT, in the hope of helping me acquire the ability to communicate smoothly with people from different backgrounds.

A Great Encouragement

I had never expected that New York City would give me such a refreshing experience. The GLT is one of the fascinating programs administered by the Center for Asia Leadership Initiatives (CALI). In seventeen days, we visited top universities, tourist attractions and famous organizations in New York City, Washington, D.C. and Boston. We visited top universities, tourist attractions and famous organizations. One of the Trek's objectives is to broaden our horizons. While I was very excited to see the schedule in New York City, I was also skeptical because I had already visited some of the places. On the flight to JFK Airport, I was thinking. 'Which aspect of New York City will be able to broaden my horizon?' I knew that my first visits to new places were what would give me the most impactful memories, and I did not expect to learn a lot by walking around the city and visiting tourist attractions. Instead, I resolved to try to learn something when we visited new places, such as non-profit organizations and the United Nations Headquarters.

Arriving at JFK Airport, I met Mr. Lim and two other students from Cambodia and Malaysia. It was my second time meeting Mr. Lim, as I had participated in the Trilateral Leadership Summit III (TLS) a few weeks earlier. It was also my second time traveling to New York City. So I felt I was quite familiar with the city.

We took a taxi to the YMCA, our accommodation during our stay there. On the way, Mr. Lim asked the driver, 'Which country are you from?' He answered, 'Ghana.' It was just small talk, but it reminded me of the fact that the taxi driver I had encountered during my first New York City trip was also from an African country. I noticed that a lot of the taxi drivers at the airport were African-Americans. Although I had an image in my head of most taxi drivers in New York City being black men, I suddenly felt that it was strange to me, as I had never seen a similar situation in Japan—one racial group dominating a particular occupation.

During our stay in New York City, we visited many famous spots, including the Statue of Liberty, the Empire State Building, the Metropolitan Museum, the Cloisters, and the United Nations Headquarters. In order for us to visit all of these places, we used the subway as our main mode of transportation. Besides using the subway, we walked very long distances every day. It sometimes exhausted me, but it was worth it because I was able to witness another situation which does not exist in Japan: people sleeping in filthy clothes while others in elegant dresses and suits passed by, all on the same street.

Now, what made these moments unforgettable? I asked myself this question again and again. Recalling my home city, I finally found an answer. First, we do not have many immigrants or other races in Japan. Therefore, I found it surprising that jobs in New York City are separated by race, as this does not happen in Japan. The other factor is that we do not have as much disparity in living standards as we saw in the U.S. Although disparity is becoming a serious issue in Japan, it is still incomparable to that of the U.S. I barely see any disparities or inequalities on the streets of Japan. That is why I was shocked to see highly privileged and disadvantaged people at the same time on the same street. I could never imagine seeing such a scene in my country.

For some time, I thought, 'It must be impossible for these people to have the right to choose their jobs.' Then, on our last day in New York City, a number of people refuted this assumption. When I visited the Supreme Court and Family Court in Brooklyn, I met Justice Ruth Shillingford. I was impressed by her background of growing up in a challenging situation as an immigrant child. She always looked confident when she spoke. My experience at the Court taught me that anything is possible and that anyone can achieve their dream if they work hard for it. We later visited a non-profit organization called Open Society, in which I met a lot of working professionals who came from underprivileged regions of Brazil, Peru and other countries. They explained that they had acquired their ambitions to improve public issues because of the hardship they experienced as children. Meeting those wonderful people who strove to fulfil their dreams, I came to believe in the possibilities the future holds. Their stories encouraged me to believe in myself although I was still unsure whether it was the right decision to further my studies abroad. Thanks to them, I am now more motivated than ever to work hard, and I believe my efforts will be rewarded someday.

The experiences in New York City definitely broadened my horizons, as they allowed me to gain a positive viewpoint through the meaningful conversations I had with the successful people we met. The Trek gave me the opportunity to discover differences from my country and to gain a better understanding of those aspects. The Trek also helped me gain insight into what was different between the U.S. and my country and to be confident in whatever decisions I make. My first Trek experience really affected me, as much as if it were my first visit to the City That Never Sleeps.

Becoming Sociable

After staying four days in New York City, we moved to Washington, D.C., which was, unexpectedly, a very familiar sight for me. I was surprised to see that the U.S. capital looks like my hometown, Narita. Unlike New York City, there were clean streets and subways, paved roads and a tranquil atmosphere. Before arriving, I had assumed that D.C. would have as many tall buildings as New York City. However, that was a misconception: in D.C., buildings are not tall and garish. Also, the roads are much wider compared to those in New York City. For these reasons, I felt relieved as soon as I arrived in D.C.

Among the numerous organizations, museums and other famous spots we visited in D.C., a dialogue at Atlas Corp was one of the most interesting experiences for me. At first I did not know much about Atlas Corp and had no idea about their missions. Later I found out from the Fellows from Australia, Venezuela, Turkey and Pakistan who work at Atlas Corp that it is a non-profit organization aiming to address social issues, including human trafficking. As part of their mission, they connect Fellows with various organizations, so that both of them can benefit from the collaboration. In order to become a Fellow, you need to quit your current job or take a year-long sabbatical. However, all the Fellows I met said that they were happy to have been given the opportunity to gain such an enriching experience. They also believe that the work experience and networks that they have gained will be beneficial when they return to their home countries. This was eye-opening for me; I did not know there was such an organization, one that would provide its Fellows with opportunities to apply their skills and knowledge in the workplace as well as enabling them to establish professional networks that will be useful in the future. I learned about the importance of establishing and maintaining contacts so that I can contribute to society by taking advantage of my knowledge, experience and connections. Good communication skills are essential in building and nurturing your network. Fortunately, the

Trek provided me with a perfect environment to develop my communication skills.

In the middle of our stay in D.C., we had a dinner meeting with a research associate of Hager Associates and her friends from different fields. During the meeting, I talked with one of her friends, Mr. Jae Yun, who worked at a real estate agency. At first, I was nervous to strike up a conversation with him, as I thought his interest was in real estate and I was not familiar with that topic. However, my concern was unnecessary. His questions were all about me, and so they were easy to answer. Thanks to him, I began to feel close with everyone there. It may sound like a normal thing to have a simple conversation over dinner. However, I was very impressed with his positive attitude toward a stranger. Although I have had conversations with experienced working professionals in Japan, many of them preferred to talk about themselves, especially their experiences in their early lives, or their fields of interest. Therefore, I usually played the role of listener. They did not seem to be interested in others, even though they asked me questions about my favorite things and my ambitions. In contrast, Mr. Jae Yun asked me a lot of questions and gave me an opportunity to explain about myself, which enabled me to be open and share my thoughts with him. I now understand that the key to having a great conversation is to ask simple questions that people like to answer. Additionally, he gave us a tip on how to enhance our communication skills. At the end of the dinner, he told us that finding common points will help us to have meaningful conversations. I thought it was a great way to not only start a conversation but also to keep the conversation going.

In D.C., I had another unforgettable experience, at the Asia Foundation. We met the Vice President of the Asia Foundation and two other people from Hager Associates. I was especially impressed by Mr. Barry M. Hager. When I introduced myself to him, he said, 'Happy birthday.' Then he added, 'Is your family okay?' Just before our visit to the Foundation, a huge typhoon had hit the mainland of Japan. I was astonished that he asked about the typhoon and knew about the latest news from Japan. While many of us think that worrying about others is normal and that we should always care about them, it is difficult to express our concern to strangers. In Japan, many people are hesitant to express their personal feelings to strangers. I felt that Mr. Hager was a very sociable person with admirable qualities. I was impressed by his broad knowledge of current issues, which allowed him to communicate with people from other countries. Meeting with Mr. Hager taught me the importance of having a positive attitude toward strangers and a vast general knowledge that will help me communicate with anyone, regardless of their background. I believe these will be very important skills to have when I am establishing and nurturing my network in a foreign land. It is much better to have an extensive knowledge of various topics, even if the knowledge is shallow. You may be surprised by how much it can help you make good conversations with people from various backgrounds.

Conclusion

Through the GLT, I learned some life lessons that I could never have gained by going on a group tour. Experiencing and observing how Americans live and work gave me a glimpse into their culture, which helped me to imagine what it would be like to live in the cities we visited. Most importantly, I acquired two invaluable lessons from the Trek. First, I learned to have confidence in my decisions and to work hard toward achieving my goals. Second, I learned that I should have the courage to speak to strangers by asking simple questions and finding common points to keep the conversation rolling. I also need to stay informed and up-to-date on current affairs, as well as expanding my knowledge on various topics so that I can talk to anyone in any situation.

Hopefully, these invaluable lessons will encourage me to take full advantage of what life has to offer. I now believe in the importance of networking and aim to establish a strong network for myself, which will be an important tool in realizing my dream of becoming a people-friendly scientist.

| Chapter 11 |

My American Dream

Amirhossein Rahbari

● ●●

The Big Bang

In life, all of us go through different experiences. Not all the experiences are good, and not all are bad. Either way, it is important for us to reflect on our experiences in order for us to learn and evolve. In the words of James Joyce, 'Mistakes are portals of discovery,' which means we must learn from our mistakes to discover ourselves and grow as individuals. Other people may not agree with the things that we find fascinating and may see them from different perspectives. Hence, understanding the significance of an event enables us to explore the true meaning of the experience and find our real purpose in life. For me, joining the GLT in the U.S. was one of the most unforgettable experiences of my life.

I was invited to join the GLT following my participation in the enriching ALY Camp in Kuala Lumpur. I was excited but worried at the same time. The GLT was a two-week tour around the U.S. that included visits to Ivy League universities and world-renowned organizations. I was delighted because it was a once-in-a-lifetime opportunity, but I was worried that my Iranian nationality would cause some trouble, given the political conflicts at the time. However, against all odds, everything went well. The GLT not only allowed me to gain a firsthand experience of Ivy League universities, it also offered me the chance to discover important aspects of the U.S. and its people.

The main reason I was enthralled to be part of the GLT was that I wanted to visit Harvard University in person and learn everything there is to learn about it, so that I could have a clearer picture of studying at my dream university. I hoped that by learning more about their entry criteria, I would be able to land a spot there in the future.

My journey began when I arrived in New York City, a moment I will never forget. I remember the sensational feeling I had while passing the streets as we drove toward my hostel; finally, I was there, in the place dubbed the greatest city in the world. Being born into a traditional Islamic culture, I have been taught that people who do not lead a lifestyle prescribed by Islam are wrong. That was why I was fascinated by the diverse lifestyles in the U.S. and wanted so much to travel there. I had been told that it is hard to travel and survive in the U.S. But the U.S. is known as 'the land of the free,' offering myriad opportunities to everyone who works hard, regardless of background. Hence, I had high expectations when I reached New York City. Based on all the things I had heard, I wanted to experience New York City for myself and learn something new and unique.

In New York City, we managed to visit most of what the city had to offer. I checked as many things as I could off my bucket list. Our stay in New York City was not long, but it was extraordinary. We saw the sights and met with professors from reputable universities, a wish come true for any student. Meeting with the New York State Supreme Court really opened my eyes to the possibility of studying Law alongside my medical program. I thoroughly enjoyed immersing myself in the New York City experience—drinking Starbucks coffee, eating street food, riding the subway, watching street performances, eating in famous food franchises, including McDonald's (the New York edition), visiting iconic landmarks, such as Times Square and the Empire State building, and standing on the sidewalk yelling, "TAXI!" to hail a cab.

The inspiration for my bucket list came from the Hollywood movies and series I had watched over the years, which helped me improve my English and learn about American culture. I have a dream of moving to the U.S. in the future, and seeing how different everything seemed on TV made me want to experience it for myself. My bucket list consisted of small things, but they had sentimental meaning, even though they seemed far-fetched. This is human nature; we are bound to want something more when it is out of reach. To me, New York City feels like the forbidden fruit of Adam and Eve. It is filled with things I wanted but was told that I could not have or that I don't have to have.

All of my experiences in New York City were amazing, but the most significant event for me was experiencing American life. I saw the tourist attractions, monuments and museums, but nothing—and I mean nothing—beats the chance to live an American life, even if only for a short time. There were two moments that I will cherish till the day I die. The first was the drive from JFK Airport to our hostel in Brooklyn and the sweet feeling of achievement and enthusiasm of discovering a whole new world. That moment was so emotional that I couldn't fully comprehend it at the time. The city lights were something I had seen on TV. It was so close, yet so far. In the car, the only thought going through my head was: Is this a dream? In the words of Walt Disney, 'A dream is a wish your heart makes.' I was thrilled not knowing what would come next!

The second significant moment was when I stood in the middle of Times Square under the giant screens, closed my eyes and imagined the number of times I had wished to be there. I stood there and looked up. My feet hurt from walking the streets of New York City from end to end, but the beauty of the city captivated me so much that the pleasure overpowered the pain. That moment was my 'big bang,' the moment I had always wanted to see, breathe and feel for myself.

On my last day in New York City, I realized that in some ways it was like every other city I had traveled to. I loved every part of New York City, but it was not exactly what I had anticipated. It had problems, just like everywhere else. The experience made me realize something. Suddenly, my dream of going to Harvard did not sound so ridiculous anymore. As I tried everything I had been dying to try, I realized that I had not really missed out on anything. Getting to try everything for myself made me realize that the idea of moving to the U.S. was not so far-fetched at all. Before, I had thought that one of my biggest challenges would be getting to the U.S., but now that I have reached my destination, it did not seem that fascinating anymore. The problem was that I was looking for something different in the U.S., and yet it did not differ much from all the other countries

I had visited. There was nothing unique about it, and so I felt that I was one step closer to where I wanted to be. The familiar feeling made me feel at ease, knowing that my dream was not so distant anymore.

The Great Expression

Less than a week in New York City, and my curiosity was still alive. I was pleased and satisfied with the American lifestyle. I had got a taste of it, and that made me feel incredible. That being said, I was no longer imagining a fictional city. New York City taught me reality. So I did not hold out much hope that Washington, D.C. would be different to what I had seen so far. Nevertheless, it was another new experience for me. As humans, we are told not to judge a book by its cover, but if we look back at history, we will see that appearances have long deceived humanity. I too was fooled, and after New York City, I vowed to never judge something unless I had experienced it myself. People say to learn from other people's experiences, so that you do not repeat their mistakes. I believe, however, that we need to go through the experience ourselves in order to understand and learn from them.

Washington, D.C. was certainly different. It was not busy. When we went out for our first meeting, I remember looking at the streets inch by inch, trying to see what the city had to offer. It certainly had less to offer than New York City when it came to entertainment, but it provided a better standard of living than the Big Apple. The city was absolutely fascinating. My time in D.C. was really important, as it helped me to evolve and change my perspective toward life. When we visited Georgetown University, I did not expect much, but as we explored the university, I realized that it is as good as any other Ivy League school. All this while, I had the misconception that a university cannot be a prominent one if it is not an Ivy League school or did not have a top ten ranking, but Georgetown changed my mind. I had always thought that I could gain access to high quality education only by going to an Ivy League university. However, experiencing Georgetown firsthand made me feel more confident and relieved that I had more options in pursuing my studies in the U.S.

I was excited to gain many new experiences in D.C. We visited many places of interest, including almost every museum in the city, which is known as a hot spot for museums. The museums were amazing, but the best one was the Smithsonian National Air and Space Museum. The best part about D.C. is that the museums are free to the public. However, the most difficult aspect of our time in D.C. was sharing a room with eight strangers. It reminded me of the saying by Philippos, 'My best dreams and worst nightmares have the same people in them.' That sentence may sound simple, but within its words are unspoken truths, and my feelings lie there. The rule of thumb says you can't easily trust people, and I don't. But living in a room with eight people whom I did not know was what was described in Dante's *Inferno*. This was my feeling about sharing a room with eight strangers: 'A hell not for living but for suffering.' Yet I had no choice but to give in to the situation. No one likes being out of his or her comfort zone. I did not like it because it was unknown and scary. However, the situation taught me a lesson: life is not always the way you want it to be. You need to adapt to your surroundings and keep an open mind in order to enjoy the whole experience. The legendary Bruce Lee once said, 'Empty your mind, be formless. Shapeless, like water. If you put water in a cup, it becomes the cup. If you put water into a bottle, it becomes the bottle. You put it in a teapot, it becomes the teapot. Now, water can flow, or it can crash.'

During my stay in a room with eight strangers, I resorted to things I had never done before. Old habits die hard, and I must say I was reluctant at first, but I went with the flow and compromised on some matters. If this experience has taught me anything, it is that there is a solution for everything. Nothing is impossible. Getting to Harvard will be an excruciating task, but when you learn to adapt, you find solutions to problems. This trip made a profound impression on me. I have acquired invaluable skills and knowledge, and I hope that my experiences from the Trek will help me in my application to Harvard.

The Ripple Effect

Have you ever anticipated something so much that once you get it, you don't know how to feel? I had been waiting for Boston, waiting to know what it felt like to see Harvard University up close. In the words of Charles Stanley, 'Our willingness to wait reveals the value we place on what we're waiting for.'

Boston was peaceful. It seemed calmer than New York City and Washington, D.C. The city was special to me because of its educational opportunities. It is the home to Harvard and the Massachusetts Institute of Technology (MIT), as well as many other esteemed universities. I will never forget the first time I entered Harvard Yard. My heart was beating so fast that I thought it was going to jump out of my chest. I was bewildered; I could not believe I was there. The gentle breeze made the trees dance before my eyes and made everything seem extraordinary. Before I went in, I took a deep breath and waited for a moment. I wanted that image to stay in my mind forever. I closed my eyes and savored it, and I looked back at all the times I had wished for that moment. All those times studying, all the late nights spent working hard just to be where I was standing. I took a moment and let it sink in, and then I went in. As I gazed at the spacious Yard, filled with people, I could not decide where to go next. The Yard was packed with freshmen moving in, and as I looked at them carrying boxes to their dormitories, I said to myself, 'One day that will be me.'

Arriving in Boston made me very excited. When I first learned about Harvard, I had immediately felt the desire to live and study in Boston one day. So here I was, experiencing the place that I hoped to live in. I was very tired on my first day at Harvard, but the anticipation kept me awake. The forty-minute ride we took from Cambridge to the Harvard Medical School was also memorable, as I got to travel through the city. I loved the architecture and how it complemented the street designs. I loved it all. I was on cloud nine once we reached Harvard Medical School. It motivated me more than ever to study hard so that I could have the opportunity to study at the prestigious Ivy League. We passed by amazing green fields to get to the Children's Hospital, where we would meet Professor Gil Alterovitz. Meeting him was an honor for me, knowing what he has accomplished. He graduated from both Harvard and MIT in the field of Biomedicine, and he is a faculty member at Harvard. He was definitely the highlight of all the people I met throughout the Trek. Graciously he took time off from his busy schedule to have dinner with us, and it was an absolute delight. Through our conversations, I found out that Professor Alterovitz accepted interns, and it sparked my desire to seize the opportunity. He told me that he would consider giving me a chance if I met all the criteria. That would mean the world to me!

What made Boston special for me was Harvard University. Lately, many people have asked me questions like 'What makes Harvard so special?' and 'What is it with you and Harvard?' Every time, I reply, 'Because it's the best.' But I have never truly shared my story with anyone, and this book, this chapter, is the perfect opportunity for me to get it off my chest once and for all. We often think that an institute of higher learning is special because of its ranking, but to me that is irrelevant. A university is special because of what it represents, and its representatives are its students. One thing that makes Harvard so special is its diversity. People from different cultures and backgrounds all gather in the same place to pursue one simple goal: to make the world a better place. That's what Harvard stands for. It changes millions of lives in a hundred different countries by being a stepping stone for those who want to make the world a better place to live in. When its students graduate, they return to their home countries and give back as much as they can to their communities. When I was nine, I met a Harvard graduate who worked in a private hospital in Iran. He told me about his time at Harvard as well as his humble beginnings. That was when I was first introduced to Harvard, and it changed my life. Because of him, I chose to study medicine to save lives just as he did, and I hope that one day I will get to tell him how he influenced my ambition to make a difference in the world.

Boston did not need to make a perfect impression. Every moment of living in it was a perfect impression. I recently learned something that made me reflect on this chapter, my story and myself. We all know the story of Noah's Ark, but certain events prompted me to look at it from a different angle. There is one thing about it that you may not have noticed before. Noah wanted to change the world, but he had no idea how to do it, so God taught him how to make an Act of Random Kindness, or ARK. We do not have to do incredible things to change the world. Even the most insignificant thing can have a big impact. That doctor from Iran may not realize this, but he has made the biggest impact in my life.

Boston was an eye-opener. The U.S. has so much to offer. Some parts need improvement, but I can feel that this is the place for me. Knowledge is what I seek, and to achieve that goal I need to be in Boston. The GLT was one of the greatest journeys of my life. Never before have I been so exposed to so much culture and diversity. I have learned valuable lessons that will help me become a better person in the future and make well-informed decisions under pressure. Now I know what it means to be a student living abroad (and how to spend as little as possible), all thanks to this incredible Trek. The trip will be forever etched in my mind because I discovered firsthand what it is like to study at renowned and Ivy League universities in the U.S. I have gained an invaluable experience, which I believe will give me an advantage when I apply to Harvard. Sometimes we need that extra push to get on the right track, and I feel that I needed such a push. I got a kick out of visiting the universities myself. Now I feel that I am moving in the right direction in life. Throughout the Trek, I heard so much about how difficult it is to get into Harvard, but then I remembered a quote by Walter Bagehot, 'The greatest pleasure in life is doing what people say you can't do.' This has encouraged me to ignore the naysayers and follow my dreams. I have vowed that I will work hard to achieve my goals. So goodbye for now, U.S. Hopefully, I will make the cut and we will meet again next year when I am a freshman at Harvard College—fingers crossed!

I was a laid-back person before I embarked on the GLT. I knew what I wanted, but I had not done anything about it. I would always tell people, 'One day, I will be at Harvard.' That has always been my goal, but when I went on the Trek and interacted with people who have achieved what I desire, I realized that I am not doing nearly as much as I should be. It is always easy to set goals, but it is never easy to work hard for them. This trip was exactly the push I needed. Catching a glimpse of what I am trying to achieve was enough to motivate me to turn my life around. The moment I got back, I started planning ways to improve myself, and I am currently in the process of achieving my objectives. I am now learning Chinese, which I should have started two years ago—but it is never too late! I have started my SAT courses with a private tutor. Hopefully, I will achieve a perfect SAT score, increasing my chances of getting into Harvard. I have also begun learning kung fu alongside my Aikido class, and, last but not least, I have started working as a translator in a business firm. I am extremely grateful to be given the opportunity to participate in the Trek, and I am confident that it will help me to excel in my future endeavors.

Part 3

•
•

Central Asia Youth Leadership Camp

| Chapter 12 |

Every Little Step Counts

Aleksandra Kan

●●●

My Adventure in Korea

My name is Aleksandra Kan. I am a twenty-two-year-old student at the Gubkin Russian State University of Oil and Gas in Tashkent, named after the geologist, I. M. Gubkin. I study at the Faculty of Operation and Maintenance of Gas Production Facilities, Gas Condensate and Underground Storage Facilities.

Last summer, I had the chance to participate in the Central Asia Youth Leadership Camp (CALC) in Korea, co-organized by Center for Asia Leadership Initiatives (CALI) and the Korea Development Bank (KDB) Foundation, and it was one of the best experiences I have ever had! Besides gaining invaluable knowledge and insights on leadership, we managed to squeeze in some fun, including dancing, singing, horseback riding and ice skating over the course of the six-week program. We even had a musical showcase to showcase our talents and an international day to share each other's cultures and traditions.

The program ended with a five-day leadership workshop conducted by Teaching Fellows from Harvard University and was thus an opportunity of a lifetime! The sessions they held were constructive and thought-provoking, stimulating me to think and come up with new ideas. Not only did I learn a lot about myself and leadership values, I also made new friends from countries such as Kazakhstan, Kyrgyzstan, Korea, South Africa and the United States. It was enriching and eye-opening to learn about people from various cultures and backgrounds. I did not expect to forge strong ties with them in such a short time, and yet that is what happened. We often had different points of views about life in general, but that made our bonds and the experience more interesting. Now that I am back in my homeland, I miss the friends I made a lot and hope that one day we will cross paths again.

What Can I Expect from the CALC?

When I heard about the leadership program, I thought, "What will it be about? How can they teach us to be leaders?" Initially, I thought it was impossible because being a leader depends on a person's initiative. If someone wants to be a leader, he will undertake all the efforts to be one. But once the course started, my doubts and concerns were cleared away.

The program began on a Sunday, and I was extremely excited to meet the Harvard Teaching Fellows. The mere mention of Harvard is enough to get everyone's attention. Everyone knows about the Ivy

League school and its high academic standards. It was a dream come true for me to engage with the Teaching Fellows and acquire knowledge from Harvard resources.

When we entered the classroom, we were greeted by Mr. John Lim, Co-founder and Managing Director of CALI Boston. He introduced himself, and then the three other Teaching Fellows arrived. They were Ms. Lee, Mr. Tarnowski and Mr. Kralev. All of them introduced themselves by giving brief summaries of their backgrounds. For the next five days, they taught us interesting topics, such as design thinking and leadership in the business industry. They instructed us to work in teams and work together to find solutions for problems they posed during the sessions.

On the second day, we were introduced to Mr. Kim, who spoke about CALI and how the non-profit organization had come about. And on the last day, we had a question-and-answer session with the Teaching Fellows, in which they encouraged us to raise any questions that we had about the program. They were open and sincere in sharing their thoughts and experiences with us. I deeply valued their opinions and advice, and I look forward to applying what I have learned in my daily life.

Leading by Example

I attended Mr. Tarnowski's leadership lectures every day. Thanks to him, I learned about new things, such as Ethos, Pathos and Logos as modes of persuasion to convince audiences. He taught us that it is important to distinguish these three elements when telling a story because if you use Ethos—credibility—you can figure out whether other people are telling truths or lies. Logos—facts or reasons—prompts you to think, "Can I believe this story?" and with Pathos—emotional appeal—leads you to understand that a person is passionate about the topic because his or her emotions show it. Now, every time someone shares new information with me, I try to analyze it using Logos, Ethos and Pathos. Through Mr. Tarnowski's lectures, I understood how we can apply these concepts in persuasive speaking or writing. He also explained to us how Ethos, Pathos and Logos can help us improve our oratory abilities.

Mr. Tarnowski showed us a video of one of President Obama's speeches, which we listened to attentively. The video showed how charismatic President Obama was and how that helped him to gain and hold the audience's attention. Charisma is an essential leadership skill, enabling leaders to inspire their audiences and evoke emotions with their calls to action. I also learned that communication and collaboration are two important elements of persuasion.

Before the program, I had seen videos of Martin Luther King Jr. and heard about him as a wonderful orator who played a key role in the American civil rights movement. But I was truly inspired after watching a short movie of his famous speech, "I Have a Dream." Afterward, we discussed the problems that he had to face. I absolutely loved the part when he said, "We will be able to speed up that day when all of God's children, black men and white men, Jews and Gentiles, Protestants and Catholics, will be able to join hands." Today, discrimination still exists. I advise everyone to read his speech. I believe that it will have a great impact on you and will motivate you to fight for positive change in society. Moreover, in order to be a good leader, like Martin Luther King Jr., you must be able to speak eloquently to convey your key messages effectively.

Mr. Tarnowski also conducted a session on body language. I had heard about this many times before, but it was interesting to gain a Harvard Teaching Fellow's point of view on this matter. I saw an experiment demonstrating the body poses of people who are confident and the poses of those who are unsure of themselves. It was interesting to see my fellow delegates change their opinions about body language after knowing the results of these experiments. The results showed that confident people are willing to take chances and are adventurous but that those who lack confidence are the exact opposite, i.e. they are afraid to make any decisions. You can even use body language in your daily life when you interact with your family and friends. Knowing more about gestures also helps when you become acquainted with new people. For example, when you meet new people, what do you first notice about them? Behavior, appearance or the way they conduct themselves in different situations? Are they friends or enemies? One of my own experiences illustrates the value of understanding body language. If I return home and see my mother quietly sitting on a chair with her arms crossed, I know that I am in big trouble. That gesture helps me to understand her mood. So Mr. Tarnowski fortified my opinion that paying attention to gestures and body language is necessary to understanding people's intentions and thoughts.

I applaud Mr. Tarnowski's method of teaching. He was very open and did not force us to listen to his lectures. We could see that he took a lot of effort to make the lessons as interesting as possible in order to engage with the delegates. His lectures were refreshing, and we learned a lot from them, especially pointers on how to give good speeches. Thanks to him, I discovered new ways to understand people's thoughts and behavior. He also gave me the opportunity to deliver a speech, in order to share my personal story.

Adapt to Succeed

"If you have a problem, you have the solution too. There is no problem without any solution." I learned this from Ms. Lee's "Design Thinking" lectures. These were a compelling and unique experience for me because I had never worked in a group before when looking for solutions to a problem. Ms. Lee taught us how to work and think as a team and how to solve problems using our imagination. We considered questions like "How can you help people adapt to new cultures?" I felt that it was the right theme for us, as all of us were in a foreign country with an unfamiliar culture. Hence, we each needed time and assistance to adapt and adjust to the new environment.

When we tried to solve the problem given by Ms. Lee, we realized that not all of our solutions were right but that it didn't matter because the experience gave us an avenue to present our points of view. Ms. Lee taught us to make decisions in critical situations and the importance of working together in a group and listening to each other's opinions. We were assigned to come up with solutions to a problem about adaptation. The process was very tedious at times, but we were committed to completing the task. On the last day, we had to present our results through a report. If I had gotten this assignment before the CALC, I would have not understood what I was supposed to do. Try imaging a situation in which your friend from another part of the world comes to your country to study. How can you help him or her to assimilate into the new culture? In the beginning, we thought about easy solutions, such as "Talk, walk or spend more time with him." However, Ms. Lee was not satisfied with our answers; she wanted us to broaden our minds. Finally, we developed a website to help foreign students adapt to new cultures. We created a prototype of our site with complete information. Thanks to Ms. Lee's "design thinking" concept, I looked at the problem from all angles.

I will never forget Ms. Lee's fascinating tasks or getting different feedbacks from everyone in the group. Ms. Lee was sincere in listening to our ideas and gave us constructive comments. I will always remember her thoughts about students from Central Asia: "You are not afraid to tell me your ideas even if they are not right; you try to think about the problem and come to a decision. I like it." I was very happy to hear such compliment.

Suppose You Are Building a Mobile App...

Lessons from Mr. Kralev were interesting because his topics of discussion were related to the most current events happening in the world. Twenty-first-century teenagers spend all their time on their mobile phones and other gadgets; they are an integral part of our lives. In Mr. Kralev's class, we were required to create a mobile app unlike anything that already available. The assignment proved that we could cultivate creativity and be innovative if we pushed ourselves to the limit.

For four days, our team tried to come up with something extraordinary that no one else has ever thought of. It was challenging at first, when we did not have any proper direction on how to move forward.

On the first day, we worked for three hours straight but could come up with only one idea. However, on the following days, our work began to show big results. We developed and presented our app prototypes to the delegates. Overall, it was an amazing process, coming up with an app that could help people and be popular in the general population. We also learned that it is not easy to present your prototype as a developer. We were bombarded with questions from the curious audience, who wanted to know about our passion and the app's mission, about our vision for the future, about the amount of money needed to kickstart our project and the resources required to pull it off. Mr. Kralev did an excellent job explaining the basic knowledge of entrepreneurship in a short period of time. I had a chance to imagine myself as an app creator, and I was happy that my ideas were approved at the session. I hope that I will get an opportunity to push this concept into something bigger in the future. I am grateful to Mr. Kralev for sharing his knowledge and experience of business and entrepreneurship. I will definitely put it to good use.

Why Not Change the World?

My adventure in Korea taught me so much about life abroad, other cultures and other people's views. It was only a six-week journey, but it has definitely changed me for the better. It was delightful to engage with brilliant and successful people from all walks of life and to learn about their paths to success. I will always cherish their advice and will try to apply it in the real world.

Now that I am back in Uzbekistan, I am determined to help young leaders in my country by passing on the skills and knowledge gained during the CALC. There are so many talented youth in Uzbekistan. All they need are support and resources to increase their standard of living and to help them achieve their goals.

When I was in Korea, I stayed at Handong University. In each building, I saw the same sentence: "Why not change the world?" I believe that people can achieve anything they want in life. Some people give up, and some go the extra mile. We all have a choice. It is up to us to seize the opportunity to succeed. I am very thankful to the organizers of CALC because I have learned a lot about ways to achieve my life goals. It is also heartening to see that CALI promotes youth development and offers them an avenue to hone their skills.

When I talk to other people about my experience, many of them ask me questions like "So how can you be a great leader?", "What characteristics must you have to become a leader?" and "Can you improve your leadership skills?" In my opinion, if you want to be a great leader, you must have a strong character—a leader is someone who can influence a group of people with his ideas and plans and who can motivate others to follow him. A leader should be compassionate and cultured. Society has to want to follow you and choose you as a leader. After the program, I know several ways to help enhance leadership abilities. First, think creatively and hold discussions with others when you're trying to find solutions to your problems or tasks. Challenge each other's ideas when you work with a group of people. Second, do not try to solve a problem on your own if you are working in a team. You have to learn together and exchange your experiences with each other. You must find out what is good or bad for the group as a whole. The ability to give relevant advice and help other people reflects a leader's traits and personality.

I want to be a change agent and make positive contributions to the society at large. The leadership program has certainly changed me for the better, and I think many of us who participated in the program began to think differently about our purposes in life. During our group assignments, I listened to many stories that gave us windows onto problems in our society: prejudice toward people who cannot see, hear or talk; young people leaving to study abroad and not coming back, when their return would help their native country's development. These issues are connected to our present society. New problems arise every year, and we need to find sustainable solutions to manage them. Therefore, youth need to step up to the plate and be ambitious leaders. Uzbekistan youth are capable of anything, but sometimes we need support from others who are willing to share their knowledge and experiences.

Each of us matters. We all can help to change the world. So what are we waiting for? Let's do it together!

| Chapter 13 |

In Pursuit of Positivity

Anastasiia Iun

● ● ●

I experienced mixed feelings of confusion and excitement when I participated in the CALC, co-organized by CALI and the KDB Foundation. Held in Korea during the summer of 2016, the leadership program was a life-changing journey for me; I discovered four important things about myself.

First, I realized that I can drastically improve the quality of my life if I stay positive in challenging situations instead of focusing on negative thoughts. Second, I now better understand my role in this world. It is important to have a vision and purpose in life and to understand how we can create positive social change to benefit the community at large. Third, my personality and characteristics make me unique. Finally, the world is interdependent and interconnected. I discovered through the program that everything I do in life, no matter how big or small it is, has a significant impact and directly affects the world around me. This journey of self-discovery brought greater meaning to my life. It has boosted my self-confidence, and now I feel empowered to help others and make this world a better place to live in.

I have just finished the first year of my Master's degree program in Counseling Psychology. I am studying at the best university in my motherland, Kyrgyzstan. I spent two years as a behavioral psycho-therapist, working with autistic children. I also learned Korean for a couple of months to find out more about my Korean heritage. People told me that I was living a fulfilling and comfortable life. However, I wasn't satisfied and felt that something was lacking. I was eager to find my place in the world, but I couldn't find any answers. I almost gave up, thinking it was an impossible task.

The result was that I was emotionally drained at that time. I was tired and didn't see any bright prospect of my future. I had planned the normal route after graduation—to finish my Master's degree and continue working as a regular psychologist. I suppose this is what some people become accustomed to in life, embracing an existing life-style with no motivation to achieve greater things in life. I did not feel that way, however. I felt empty. I wanted to get rid of the emptiness, but unfortunately, I did not know how. I tried to solve the problem by repeatedly asking myself questions: "What am I doing here? Why? What is the reason? What is next? Is this how I will live my life, the life that is too short to waste?" These questions really bothered me.

As you can see, it was a confusing and mind-boggling period in my life. To put it in a simpler way, I didn't know how I could help my community. Although I knew I wanted to do something important in the education field, I couldn't think of a way to contribute, and I didn't know which area to focus on. There are already plenty of bright people in the education field who are influential and have made wonderful contributions in their line of work. How can I beat that or even catch up to their level? Am I brave enough to carry out such important work? Do I have the capabilities?

Luckily, in March 2016, my Korean teacher told me about a program to study Korean language and culture in Korea. I applied for the program and was chosen to participate in the course during the six-week summer period. Later in May, I was invited to go to the University of Massachusetts Boston, in the United States, as a visiting research scholar for a semester.

I thought, 'Wow! This is probably what I need right now: a change, even if it's only for a short period of time.' I hoped that going to another place with an unfamiliar environment would do me good. I believed that it would allow me to meet people from different backgrounds and enable me to listen to their thoughts and ideas. Hopefully, it would help me answer the questions still lingering in my mind.

I was also excited and happy to go to Korea because I was keen to learn more about my identity. As an ethnic Korean of partial Russian descent, I represent two minority groups in Kyrgyzstan, and I had trouble fitting in with the Kyrgyz community, since I am so different from many of them. I am both Korean and Russian, so how do I need to behave? Do I need to behave like a Russian or like a Korean? Who am I? As a minority member of society, can I feel at home in Kyrgyzstan? If yes, then how can I help my country develop and prosper?

I thought that by embracing my roots in Korea and learning more about the people and culture there, I would be able to find my true identity. When the summer began, I went to Korea with high hopes of finding my answers. I was open to adventures. The program promised to provide a lot of rich new experiences, and I was excited to have any experiences that would help to deal with my burn-out.

The Korean language and culture program was intensive and interesting. Every day, there was something exciting to learn. I met new and diverse people. Some of them became my good friends. Moreover, I did a lot of things I had never done before back in Kyrgyzstan. I dyed scarves, made toys, cooked traditional Korean food, danced K-pop, sang K-pop and did lots of other things. We visited historical places as well as relevant modern attractions. I felt that the time I spent there was much more than just one and a half months. We had done so many things that I felt that we must have been there for at least half a year or even more.

I liked Korean culture a lot. The local Koreans were very polite and ready to help us. I also met a lot of people like me, people with a Korean heritage but greatly influenced by Russian and Central Asian culture. I felt that I had finally found my group.

There was only one sad thing occupying my thoughts all the time: I still felt down, upset, insecure, heavy, slow and purposeless. There was a tightness inside me. I did not feel whole as a person; instead I felt fragmented. I had always thought that something was wrong with my emotional state. Of course, I experienced moments of happiness like any other person, but they were not as frequent as I wanted them to be, and I did not know how to keep them. I did not know how to make them last longer.

I wanted desperately to change these feelings and overcome my negative thoughts. I wished that I could view and interpret things as they truly were and not allow them to hurt me so much and bring me so much distress. I felt that it would be wonderful to be at peace with myself and to find some meaning in my life.

Fortunately, the program I was in included leadership training as part of its curriculum. We were supposed to start the training near the end of the program, with Harvard graduates as our trainers.

I anticipated those classes with some thoughts that for me were unusual: "Wow! Is it really me participating in such training? It can't be real!" I had always doubted that such classes were for me. I assumed that they were only for exceptional people who were born to be leaders and who strongly believed that they are real leaders. I certainly didn't consider myself exceptional. I would have been glad to become a leader one day, but I was sure I did not have all the qualities of a good leader. Thus, I came to the conclusion that the leadership classes were definitely not meant for me.

Still, I waited for them with interest and curiosity. Maybe this curiosity was what has helped me to explore and achieve things in life. Perhaps this curiosity helps me step forward and try new things.

The feelings I experienced during our five-day leadership training will forever be imprinted in my memory. They stirred up everything inside of me. I didn't notice when I first began to experience new emotions, like hope and enthusiasm, during the session. Those emotions had not been frequent guests for me, but eventually they stood up so clearly in my mind that it was impossible to dismiss them. I still remember their unusual influence. They gave me support, confidence and security. And when I was in that positive emotional state, I felt energized. I felt how light my body was. I was open and free. I felt productive, as if I could do a lot of things. I loved those feelings. I wanted to experience them over and over again.

Sometimes I caught myself thinking how lucky I was to be participating in the leadership classes. My mere presence at the training and listening to the material about leadership made me think that I was capable of becoming a leader. It gave me hope.

The trainers' unique personalities contributed to the myriad positive emotions I experienced during the classes. They were kind, generous, focused and positive. I particularly enjoyed Mr. Tarnowski's classes. He was passionate about the content of the classes, and he was energetic, moving from one place to another around the room to engage with all of us and ensure that we really understood the material. He looked at us with great interest. He listened to us with concern and empathy. He was open to our thoughts and views. We felt a sense of belonging and of being heard and valued. I later learned, in another class, that this is called a resonant relationship. If leaders can activate a positive emotional state in the people who look up to them, the leaders can then empower those people. In other words, the leaders create a secure atmosphere that empowers others to grow, and this in turn leads to the people becoming confident and creative.

For me, the most important things in the program ended up being the feelings and emotions I experienced during the leadership classes, rather than the material itself. The same material is available everywhere, but it is difficult to find teachers like the Harvard trainers. The same material could have been taught differently. I was very lucky to meet such wonderful trainers, who taught the material in their own unique way.

After the program, I decided to work on my emotional state, in order to experience those same invigorating feelings on a more regular and stable basis. Almost three months have passed since I made that decision, and I now feel completely different. I find time for myself. I sleep well and feel more balanced inside. I am happy and enjoy life more. I am productive and have better relationships with the people around me. I have realized the importance of tuning in to one's emotions and taking better care of oneself. I am also more confident in the things that I do. My quality of life has improved tremendously, to such extent that I never want to go back to where I used to be, before I participated in the leadership program. At last, I feel that my life is heading in the right direction.

When I started to experience a more stable positive emotional state, I remembered that Mr. Kralev, one of the Harvard Teaching Fellows, said that it was important to have a vision for a company or a product that one is designing for the market. I paused and started to think about my life as if it were a product. What was my personal vision for my life? Isn't that the most important thing one can think about? These questions pushed me to search for additional sources of information about vision construction. I started to take some wonderful classes on leadership and emotional intelligence. If we had not covered the importance of vision with Mr. Kralev, I wouldn't have searched for this information after the program was over, and I would never have been able to create my own vision.

It took me a long time even to sketch out my vision, but now I know what I want to do. The best contribution I can make in this life is to become a coach and help people in my country run organizations, schools, clinics and other institutions. If I become a good coach, I will have an opportunity to help more people, because people with managerial positions who come to my sessions will interact with other people from different levels, and they in turn will interact with other groups of people. If I help at least one person, let's say a school principal, to become a more effective leader, the children, their parents, their teachers and other employees at the school will all benefit from my leadership. The quality of their lives will be changed for the better. People will be happier, and they will be more willing to help others to be better and more educated. Hopefully, they will help to contribute to the development of my home country. They will help the country, its people and humanity as a whole to prosper. I know now that I should think about the global impact of the behavior of one single person. I alone cannot change the world, but I can change a lot of people for the better. As it says in the Talmud, 'And whoever saves a life, it is considered as if he saved an entire world.'

Exploring these thoughts and feelings, I came to understand that I should value both my heritages, Korean and Russian. Yet I am more than just Korean and Russian. I am human. This is the most important thing. I am a human being who wants to help other people, and that is more important than finding out what my 'real' ethnic identity is. For people like me, with mixed-race ancestry, it is sometimes crucial to look at the bigger picture of all humanity. On that level, you can find a common language with other people, a way of communicating between one human being and another human being. This was my third discovery. A person with a mission is more than just a member of one ethnic group.

Those thoughts led me to my fourth discovery. Everything I did, everything that I am doing and everything that I will do in the future has meaning and significance. Everything that happens to me has meaning and significance. I do not feel purposeless anymore.

I set several goals in line with my vision. First, I am not going to ignore my emotional self anymore. I am not going to neglect myself. I will take care of myself. If I do, I will be fresh, resourceful and ready to take care of other people. As a future counselor and coach, I cannot be careless, inattentive and unthoughtful toward my clients. It would be a violation of the ethics code. It would be a violation against humans. I must always be in shape if I want to be a helpful, useful and significant person.

I have been careful to capture the data and learn when I feel good and balanced. I feel good when there is humor in my life, when I have enough sleep, when I engage in my hobbies, when I talk and listen to people, when I dare to do new things and when I make mistakes and take them as lessons, feeling grateful to them as a result. I feel good, balanced and whole when I put effort into building close and sincere relationships with people. I feel whole and content when I am open to the people around me. I feel whole when I see or do kind things, when I am grateful and just. I feel good when I am open to new things and when I find pleasure in the simple things in life. I feel good and lifted when I do sports. Even simple and short exercises make my day nicer. I feel good, self-sufficient and secure when I do not wait for other people to help alleviate my distress. When I can do it by myself, I feel more empowered and independent. When I take care of myself, I feel human. I develop a greater sense of self-respect. I have no need to blame other people around me. I truly believe that only by recognizing, accepting, learning and being able to manage one's emotional state of mind can one help others.

I study more seriously now. I am more eager and focused on my studies. It has become clearer now what I need to do and learn, and why. It is not a burden but an opportunity to achieve my purpose in life—to help people. As I said, everything that is happening to me now is a valuable experience and will help me to understand other people better. Everything that happens to me shapes me into a person with deep thoughts and feelings.

Currently I am in Boston, writing a story about one of the most influential moments in my life. Sometimes you find solutions to important problems in unfamiliar places. Sometimes you meet people who change your life so dramatically that you will never forget them.

I feel very lucky that the events in my life happened the way they did. Thanks to them, I went to Korea to meet people whose behavior and lectures had such a great impact on me that my life has now changed for the better. From an insecure person with no vision, struggling with ethnic identity crisis, I turned into a person with vision, purpose and goals. I feel more secure and confident. I have a greater sense of accomplishment because I have learned to embrace a positive attitude and mindset. This allows me to stay grateful, humble and calm. It has enhanced my overall well-being, and now I feel much happier and healthier.

I would like to express my gratitude to CALI and the KDB Foundation for giving me the opportunity to participate in the CALC. I am truly honored and privileged to have been given the chance to write about one of the best episodes in my life, the episode in which I met great people and discovered myself. I will never forget this experience. I hope that CALI will continue to help others find their purpose and vision in life. I believe that the program will benefit more people in the future and will change the lives of those in need.

| Chapter 14 |
New World, New Me

Anjela Kamalova

● ● ●

Do you believe that you can change the world? I do. When I was a kid, I wanted to become the President of my country, Uzbekistan, a country with a long history, situated in Central Asia. I knew that to make my dream come true I would need to study hard. Later, I realized that becoming the President would be very difficult, and so I decided that I wanted to become a doctor instead. As I grew older, I came to understand that being a doctor is a highly challenging job and that doctors are responsible for their patients' well-being. Sometimes, doctors' decisions can make the difference between life and death. Therefore, I changed my mind again and decided to become a teacher; I thought it would be much easier to teach people. I even had a chance to try it out: when I was a second-year university student, I took a part-time job as a Russian teacher at a language centre. At first, I thought I was doing well; I tried different methods to teach my students. But as time passed, I did not see any progress. I tried changing my teaching methods, but they were still unsuccessful. After that, I gave up the idea of becoming a teacher and could not decide on my future ambition. I stopped believing that I would be able to make an impact in this world. I lost both my self-confidence and my driving force to pursue any goals in life.

Then, in June 2016, I went to Korea as part of the six-week CALC, co-organized by CALI and the KDB Foundation in Pohang, Korea. My ancestors are Koreans, and I wanted to visit their homeland in the hopes of finding my roots there. I was excited to study in Korea, to learn about the culture and experience the lifestyle. Furthermore, I was really looking forward to the five-day Leadership program after finding out that the Teaching Fellows were from Harvard University. Even before the program started, I was already excited to meet with such a great group of people and to learn new things from them. I also hoped that, during the workshops, I would learn how to believe in myself again.

Following my participation in the CALC, I wanted to prove to myself that I could make a difference in this world and that change was possible. So when CALI offered me the chance to write a chapter on my experience during the program, I jumped at the opportunity without any hesitation!

Although I was enthusiastic, I was a little afraid to attend the workshops. There were thirty-two delegates in total, from Central Asian countries including Kazakhstan, Uzbekistan and Kyrgyzstan. We were divided into six groups. My group consisted of five people, and I was chosen as the group leader. It felt like a burden and a big responsibility. I remembered that when I was in junior and secondary school I had been chosen as team leader numerous times. Back then,

I was confident in my abilities and tried to get the job done by myself so that our team would succeed. But it was a different story this time around. I hadn't any idea what we would be doing during the workshops and lectures. Additionally, I knew that everything would be conducted in English, and I did not think that my level of English would be good enough for me to lead my group effectively. Fortunately, the first day of the workshops went smoothly, and my group mates cheered me on to do my best. I felt relieved, and their support spurred me to carry on.

On the first day, we met with our Teaching Fellows. They briefed us about the program module, and also shared their life stories with us before the sessions started. They were an interesting and fun bunch of people. Their personal stories were fascinating, and I was very surprised by how honest and open they were with us. After hearing them, I felt that it was going to be an enthralling program.

The first lecture was Design Thinking with Ms. Lee. First of all, she taught us how to find the best solution to any problem. In one exercise, we created a sketch of a football field for blind people and tried to develop a safe solution to help an elderly woman clean her house. At first glance it seemed very hard because we had to find simple and affordable solutions that would cater to everyone. But Ms. Lee was very reassuring and showed us that there are easy ways to solve even difficult problems. After that, we were given the main task for Design Thinking, which was relatable for all of us. We had to look for the best ways to help foreign students adapt to new cultures. To begin, we exchanged stories about our own experiences of living abroad and the difficulties we faced. It was ironic that all of my group members had experienced similar problems: financial challenges, language and cultural barriers, and a lack of familiarity with the different food and climate. Together, we decided to choose one of these problems, which we thought might resonate with the students. We chose the language barrier, but we wanted to be specific, so we focused on students who have theoretical knowledge of the language spoken in the foreign country but are still faced with a language barrier because they have never practiced speaking it.

We then proceeded to work as a group to find a solution. It was tough at first because we had never done such an assignment before, but Ms. Lee was very helpful, taking us through the task step by step so that we could come up with the best solution. The exercise was fascinating; each of us were there in a foreign land and all of us had faced challenges in communicating with the locals. We recalled Ms. Lee's first exercise, which required us to find solutions that would help everyone regardless of how much money they had. We brain-stormed for quite a while and came up with various solutions. We thought about each solution from different angles. Ms. Lee told us not to think too much about it and just to write down the ideas and thoughts that came naturally to us. She was right. All of a sudden the right decision came to us. We decided to set up a Drama Club for the students. It would help the students to meet new people and would allow them to imagine themselves as actors. We chose this solution because when we first arrived in Korea for the program, we partook in a musical, and it helped us to become friends and to improve our public speaking skills.

We carefully thought about every detail to make our idea feasible, basing a lot of them on our own experiences. On the final day of the CALC, we presented our solution to everyone in class. The other teams, as well as Ms. Lee, gave us their feedback. Some thought that our solution was good, while others found many disadvantages. But, in my opinion, Design Thinking is more focused on working and thinking about the problem together than on finding the actual solution. We did not use the internet or any other resources. We worked on it for only a short period of time. Even though we did not have much time to think, we felt that our ideas were effective and that we could work well as a team.

Mr. Kralev conducted a compelling workshop on Entrepreneurship. Initially, I was more worried about this workshop than about the other sessions because I knew nothing about entrepreneurship, and I thought I would face difficulties in understanding the topics of discussion. However, Mr. Kralev made it easy for everyone to comprehend the subject. He introduced us to the traits of successful entrepreneurs, such as passion, resilience, a strong sense of self, flexibility and vision. Our task was to create a business plan. We took several days to come up with ideas for a new mobile app, its economic statement and ways to gain profit from it.

Our group had many ideas about the type of app that we wanted to make, but some of them already existed, while others were not good enough. We wanted to create something that was refreshing, useful and easy to use. We discussed each suggestion and asked for advice and feedback from other groups. Finally, we decided to go with the idea of an Education app that would enable teachers to teach their subjects online and earn money at the same time. Students could pick a subject of their choice and the suitable teacher for it. When we presented our ideas to the class, we received a mixture of positive and negative feedback, as well as a lot of questions. One of the students even told us about the existence of such an internet site. So we tried to improve our app. We also discussed the app's vision, mission, service, design, operations and finances. We took all the comments and questions that had been raised into account to enhance our business plan. In the end, even though our app, named 'Search & Match' did not win the best business idea, we were happy and satisfied because we had worked well as a team, as we developed our own entrepreneurial ideas for the first time. Everyone contributed their thoughts, and we listened to each other's suggestions. It was a fun session that provided us with a chance to go inside the mind of an entrepreneur.

The last few lectures, by Mr. Tarnowski on Leadership Communications, were more or less familiar to me. I had participated in a public speaking contest at my university back home. I have always been afraid to speak in public because I tend to forget what I want to say and ramble. However, I decided to try public speaking during my second year at university to overcome my fear. As I was majoring in Japanese, I wanted to improve my proficiency in the language by participating in a Japanese-language public speaking contest. I was determined to win and prepared intensively with my Japanese lecturers for a month. We worked on my text, accent, intonation, pauses and eye contact to improve my performance. When the day finally came, I was excited and ready to take the stage. I had the speech ready, but when I went up on stage and looked out at the sea of people watching me in silence, I froze up and started to stumble over my words. Eventually I managed to finish my speech, but I did not win any prizes. Still, my lecturers were not disappointed in me. I felt ashamed for quite a long time, but I took it as a lesson and decided to give it another shot the following year. During my third year, I was much better prepared because I did not want such an embarrassing incident to happen again. I did not forget the speech that time around and took fourth place.

Mr. Tarnowski's workshops reminded me of that time and gave me new inspiration. I learned how to use Ethos (credibility or character), Pathos (emotions) and Logos (facts). We listened to the stories of famous people and shared our personal stories with everyone in the class. Mr. Tarnowski taught us ways to identify Ethos, Pathos and Logos in other people's stories. He always mixed up our groups so that we worked with different delegates in every lesson, which enabled me to share my story with delegates from many different backgrounds, and also to listen to theirs. I thought it was amazing that people have such different opinions and ways of thinking. I was deeply impressed by every story I heard. I was glad that all thirty-two students could share their stories with each other. I think we became closer during these lectures. On the last day of the CALC, five students, including me, delivered speeches about the changes that we wanted to make in the world.

Now that I know more about public narrative, I will definitely use it in my home country at my next public speaking contest and share my experiences at the CALC with the audience. The things I learned there taught me a lot about life. I got a chance to hear amazing stories about Harvard Professors and Teaching Fellows' lives, and they in turn were interested to know more about the delegates. I am very fortunate to have met such great people. My interactions with them made me realize that I too have my own life story. Even though it is not perfect, I own it and I can create my own episodes in my life journey. Meeting with Mr. Kim, Mr. Lim, Ms. Lee, Mr. Tarnowski and Mr. Kralev influenced me to change my worldview within the course of only a few days. Their stories made me believe in myself. The experience inspired me to be better. I realized that I do not want to become a desk jockey; instead I want a job that will allow me to communicate with other people and help my country to prosper. Although I still don't know how to achieve my goal, I know that I want to be someone great.

Although Uzbekistan is quite a young country, it is steeped in tradition, which I think is important for every nation. Nevertheless, people should keep up with the times. For example, many people in Uzbekistan marry too early, and arranged marriages are still common. In many Uzbek families, when a child turns eighteen, his or her parents will start to plan a marriage. Parents will choose partners for their children. Even if the sons or daughters already have someone they love, their parents will not allow them to marry those partners if they disapprove of the relationship. I want the older generation to stop interrupting the private lives of younger people. At the same time, in my opinion, both parents and children should think about education first. We need to change people's mindsets and make education a priority. Michelle Obama once said to an audience of teenage girls, "There's no boy at this age that is cute enough or interesting enough to stop you from getting your education. If I had worried about who liked me and who thought I was cute when I was your age, I wouldn't be married to the President of the United States today."

The first President of Uzbekistan, Islam Karimov, emphasized that the youth of Uzbekistan are our future, our support and our hope. I think every country can relate to this. The youth are energetic, vibrant and filled with brilliant ideas. The CALC in Korea showed me that youth everywhere have a great deal to offer and are more than capable of being leaders. We have an integral role to play in changing the world for the better. Previously, I had thought that great people were born great, but now I understood that in order to become great, we need knowledge, self-confidence and a dream to succeed.

| Chapter 15 |

Inspiring Greatness

Evgeniy Kim and Zarina Shemdanova

● ● ●

Evgeniy Kim

What Motivates You?

Motivation is an essential element if you want to achieve your goals in life. Without the desire to succeed, you will get nowhere. The proof of this is that some people will do whatever it takes to accomplish their dreams, while those who are 'all talk and no action' spend a lot of time boasting but accomplish little.

How do I define motivation? For me, it is a feeling that allows me to understand the reasons behind my actions. It helps people to believe in themselves, and this belief generates success. I am a student from Uzbekistan with ambitions, goals, beliefs and dreams. I consider myself a highly motivated person, since everything I have achieved so far is due to my yearning to get things done and move one step closer to achieving my goals.

You can find motivation everywhere; it can come from your parents, friends or even strangers who inspire you to take action. I recently joined the CALC, co-organized by CALI and the KDB Foundation in Korea. The KDB Foundation is a unique organization that operates in countries such as Uzbekistan, Kyrgyzstan and Kazakhstan, besides Korea. The program was one the most memorable experiences of my life. It showed me how motivation can influence my personal growth and help me to attain my goals.

I was a fourteen-year-old boy without any purpose in life when I started learning Korean. I still remember that moment. An unfamiliar elderly woman came to our class to make an announcement about free Korean language courses. Many questions popped into to my mind: 'Can I really learn Korean?', 'I am Korean, so I have to know this language' and 'Wow, it is free!' So I started the course together with a friend. Later I moved to another district, but that did not stop me from continuing to learn Korean.

Soon after that, I received a phone call from my friend. 'Can you imagine?' he exclaimed. 'I have been accepted to attend a college in Seoul, Korea, for free!' I was surprised and depressed at the same time; I regretted not applying to any colleges in Korea after finishing my Korean course. However, I refused to let it bring me down. The conversation with my friend sparked my motivation to take up another Korean language course at the Sejong Korean School and then at the Culture and Education Center of Korea, both in Tashkent, so that I could get a refresher on Korean as well as gaining basic knowledge about Korean culture.

A Dream Come True

At the beginning of March, we were informed about the CALC, which provided an opportunity to local Koreans to learn the Korean language as well as to familiarize themselves with Korean culture and traditions. Without hesitation, I submitted all the required documents to the program head, Mr. Seonhan Kim. I went through the interview process and was thrilled to be accepted! Although the program aimed to enhance students' ability to speak Korean and broaden their minds about Korean history and culture, it also provided us with a platform to participate in a myriad of activities, meet new friends and be part of an unforgettable experience.

Humidity and fog greeted me at the Incheon International Airport, together with thirty-one other delegates from three countries—Uzbekistan, Kazakhstan and Kyrgyzstan. Someone shouted, 'Welcome!' and we saw a row of smiling faces greeting us as if we were their best friends. It was delightful to see the locals caring about our well-being in their home country. We took a group photo, and from that moment we became a family. Everybody was sincere; we could see as much on their faces. I could not believe that I was actually in Korea for the program. I had to pinch myself to make sure it was not a dream.

Fast Friends

To be honest, I was worried about not being able to make friends in the program because everyone, including delegates from my country, came from different institutions of higher learning. I was afraid that the others would form social cliques and that no one would want to befriend me. However, that feeling quickly disappeared after I got to know the delegates. Sergey Kim, Aleksey Lyan, Zarina Shemdanova, Ekaterina Kim, Angelina Starkova and Elena Em all embraced me as part of their group.

They were very friendly, and I was impressed by their kindness, humor and open-mindedness. We supported each other in different situations, especially in difficult moments. I was truly touched by their personalities and admirable character traits. Unfortunately, it was impossible to participate in every activity together, since we were divided into four groups according to our proficiency in the Korean language. However, we gathered to eat together and catch up at every meal throughout the program. It was amazing how quickly we became fast friends.

First Lessons

Orientation Day marked the start of the program. On the first day, I had my breakfast at 'Mom's Kitchen' with the rest of the delegates and staff. I will never forget the friendly and kind-hearted elderly woman who greeted me that morning at breakfast. She had a cute smile and asked me what I wanted to have. At that moment, I fell in love with the place, thanks to the nice people, inviting atmosphere and delicious meals. I will always remember my first breakfast there, eating food made with love. 'Wow, it is toast with cinnamon!' said Sergey. 'Yes, I have never tried this before,' Zarina answered.

After breakfast, we headed for our first Korean language lesson. We were excited, though we did not know what to expect. 'Hello!

My name is Choi Yebin, and I will be your teacher during these six weeks in Handong!' She smiled whenever she talked. Her mannerisms showed positive energy and kindness, and I knew that she would make a great teacher and would make our lessons fun and exciting. I was confident that we would gain a lot of knowledge from her.

At the introductory session, I said, 'My name is Evgeniy Kim, and I am from Uzbekistan. Currently, I am a student at Westminster International University in Tashkent.' Since we were at only an elementary proficiency level, our teacher was surprised by our pronunciation and fluency. Soon we decided to skip the introductory lessons, including the introduction of the alphabet, and proceed with learning about grammar and new words at a pre-intermediate level. I also made new friends there: Yulia Ten, Anna Son, Mikhail Lee and Anastasiia Iun. I had a pleasant time learning with them. It was enjoyable and did not feel as if we were attending lessons. Together, we overcame obstacles, helped each other with homework and supported one another.

Zarina Shemdanova

Learning Outside the Classroom

The program is more than just classroom education. We went out on field trips to learn more about the local customs and traditions.

Korea is famous for its stunning temples. So you can imagine how enthusiastic I was when we went to Bulguksa Temple. The temple is the representative relic of Gyeongju and we were told that it is well-known for the artistic touch of its stone relics. The temple was designated as a World Cultural Asset by UNESCO in 1995. The ambience in the temple grounds was so peaceful and tranquil. The temple itself was gorgeous and we were mesmerized by its beauty. I wanted to touch parts of the temple to feel its energy. A couple of times, I did not withhold myself and touched its columns and doors. That gave me warmth and peace of mind. As I walked around the temple grounds, I imagined myself living during that period. I was having such an enjoyable time that it seemed that time was moving too fast. It was such a joy to have visited this wonderful historical site. Some might find it boring but it was an incredible and enriching trip for me.

Besides visiting places of interest, we were given the opportunity to witness and make local traditional products. We went to a small workshop in which an old man was busy creating and selling traditional souvenirs. Our mission was to make our own silver trinkets or necklaces. Somebody from our group joked, 'Wow! Looks like our trinkets will sell like hot cakes!' It motivated us to do our best in making our products. It was a difficult task that required accuracy and a lot of patience. Personally, I enjoy painstaking work, but accuracy and I do not mix, so I was very careful when I painted the products. We looked forward to more educational and engaging activities in store throughout the program.

That night, at 1:30 a.m., Sergei grumbled, 'I am hungry.' 'Me too!' the other five boys screamed. Then our Student Leader, Lee Hechan, said, 'Did you know that we have a late-night tradition?' He was a tall person with a kind and boyish face who wore glasses and a funny hairstyle. He asked us, 'Would you like to order chicken?' and obviously we answered, 'YES!' During our late supper, we shared our experiences with our Student Leader. Lee Hechan gave us valuable insights on living alone in Korea. We cracked jokes and became close. Lee Hechan helped us every time we needed him, and we supported him as well. One night he said that he would try to visit all three countries, Uzbekistan, Kyrgyzstan and Kazakhstan, in the winter. In return, we told him that we would invite him to try our traditional dishes when he visits. We were very excited at the thought of seeing each other again over the holiday.

At the beginning of the third week, we were shocked to be divided into groups in order to perform a musical in Korean. We had no idea about what musical direction to take and spent the next two weeks brainstorming on the concept of the musical. I was the only boy in my group of eight. There were some misunderstandings, but we took everything in stride. My teammates were a bunch of smart and creative girls. I will never forget the time spent with Elena Tyo, Ksenia Son, Anastasiia Iun, Natalya Kim, Irina Tsay, Annel Salimjanova and Yulia Lee. We were supportive of each other and worked well together. Everyone was eager to share ideas. I proposed that we perform a fairytale-based musical, and I was glad that my teammates agreed. We had a lot of fun during rehearsals every evening, even though it was exhausting after a long day attending lessons. We were committed as a team and understood that we had to stay strong in order to pull it off.

A Journey to Remember

Among the best parts of the CALC were the Leadership workshops conducted by Teaching Fellows from Harvard University. The rest of the delegates felt the same way. When I entered the classroom for the first workshop, I noticed that my name was highlighted on the board. 'What does it mean?' I asked our Student Leader. He told me that I had been chosen as a team leader. I felt proud to be picked for the role. It boosted my confidence, and I felt I was ready for everything.

From the first session, we understood that it would not be an easy program. It was designed to broaden our minds in different areas, including Entrepreneurship, Public Speaking and Design Thinking. The sessions were very intensive, but we could not wait to learn from the Harvard Teaching Fellows. We were confident that we would gain new knowledge and skills, such as effective teamwork, decision making and public speaking, as well as improving our English.

Every Teaching Fellow influenced us in a positive way. They were also open and gave us avenues to express our ideas and abilities in every session. The CALC enabled us to participate in various assignments that stimulated our minds and encouraged us to think creatively and analytically.

The workshop with Ms. Lee was interesting, useful and thought-provoking. Sometimes we discussed heartwarming scenarios that tugged at our heart strings and even make us burst into tears. For example, one task required us to solve a problem involving a boy who loved playing football. He met with a car accident and lost his eyesight. We had to find a way that would enable him to continue playing football. I thought every group did well and came up with interesting and creative solutions.

Mr. Kralev gave us a very challenging task in his workshop. We had to develop our own mobile app and present a business plan to market it. Everybody was nervous, as most of us were not familiar with the topic of discussion. However, we took up the challenge and were eager to complete the task well. Some of the projects raised during Mr. Kralev's workshop were very realistic, making us feel as if we were doing tasks in the real world. Mr. Kralev even advised us to keep our ideas so that we could try to develop them further in the near future.

Mr. Tarnowski conducted the last workshop on Public Speaking. His workshop not only taught us public speaking skills but also provoked our thoughts, as we had to speak about global issues and ways to solve them. I was impressed with Kim Vitaliy's speech about the Korean immigration issue and the difficulties they have faced in the past. He even shared his life story, describing how people judged him for his ethnicity and nationality when he was young. Additionally, he talked about scale changes in Uzbekistan, people's attitude toward others and how the whole country has improved in different fields throughout the years. He persuaded us not to leave our motherland but to try to improve the country's situation and make it better. This made me emotional and brought me close to tears. I love Uzbekistan, and to me it is the most peaceful country in Central Asia. There and then, I realized that I should do my best to contribute to my country's development. Honestly, every word from my fellow delegates and Mr. Tarnowski was valuable and motivating. 'It is a great opportunity!' This phrase was common in our group, and we learned to value every opportunity to acquire new skills. The workshop gave us the perfect platform to share our thoughts and speak about global problems on a deeper level. It gave us a chance to develop our personal characteristics and impact the world around us.

All Good Things Must Come to an End

Near the end of the Trek, we were sad and found it hard to say goodbye. The six weeks we spent together had strengthened our relationships. We became one big family with huge dreams.

I cannot describe the feelings I had when we were at the airport. It was time to leave, to say our goodbyes. I saw everyone hugging each other for the last time and taking photos as mementos. Almost everyone was crying. The environment became somber, and I could not contain myself anymore. My eyes began to brim with tears of sadness. Then the tears started streaming down my face. I could not stand seeing everyone so sad. Despite the tears, however, we managed to smile. We were happy to have met each other and to have bonded over the six-week program. We promised to keep in touch and to make an effort to visit each other's home countries. Till we meet again!

I would like to take this opportunity to thank a special person who went the extra mile to make every delegate comfortable, happy and at ease during the program: Mr. Vladimir Samsonov, from Uzbekistan. He is a great individual with a positive attitude, a kind soul, a brave heart and a beautiful personality. He was our translator during the Trek and knew every event, activity and schedule like the back of his hand. He was with us till the end, always supporting us, teaching us new experiences and sharing fun and hilarious moments with us. Mr. Vladimir, if you are reading this chapter, know that it was written with a sincere heart. You are always welcome in Uzbekistan. We are all waiting for you here! We wish you the best of luck in all your future endeavors. Take care, friend!

The summer of 2016 was the best summer of my life. The CALC

was a meaningful and unforgettable experience for all of the delegates. We gained useful skills and knowledge, and in addition we developed strong friendships and camaraderie over a short period of time. The program has ended, but it marked the beginning of a new chapter in our lives. I strongly recommend the CALC to everyone. I also urge all of you who are reading this to participate in any programs that allow you to demonstrate your leadership skills. The world needs a new generation of leaders with clear vision and direction, creativity and passion to make the world a better place for everyone.

Part 4

.
.

Trilateral Leadership Summit III

| Chapter 16 |

Embracing Change

Megumi Konishi

● ●●

'Don't settle.' This is just one fraction of a famous quote by Steve Jobs, made up of two very simple words, but it strikes a chord in my heart every time I see it.

I have always tried to avoid drastic changes in my life. I started taking violin lessons when I was five years old but became bored with it very quickly. I wanted to quit. However, I was also scared that the effort that had gone into my violin practices would go to waste, and I worried that by quitting the violin, I would somehow lose part of my identity. When I finally switched to the guitar last year, it involved a lot of stress and felt like a huge accomplishment, although to other people it might seem like a minor change. I also joined an orchestra club in my elementary school in Japan, with frequent and rigorous practices that used up a lot of my time and energy. Although I was becoming more and more busy preparing for my entrance exams, I could not quit the orchestra club because of my pride, the knowledge that I had kept it up for so long, and the fear of losing such a big part of my life. I looked at change as something negative and not worth it. And I would never have imagined that my perspective on this issue could change so much over the course of just five days.

I took part in the Trilateral Leadership Summit III (TLS) in Incheon, Korea, with fifty other delegates from three different countries. The summit comprised inspiring workshops and plenary sessions conducted by Teaching Fellows from Harvard. This was where I was able to realize just how many things the phrase 'Don't settle' can be applied to. The full quotation is about how people can only be truly satisfied if they love what they do when they are working, and how they should not settle for a job that they are not happy with. But during this five-day camp, several questions came to my mind. How does this quote connect with innovation and creation? How does it connect with leadership? How can the words 'Don't settle' be used in a more general sense?

On the second, third and fourth days of the camp, I attended Mr. Kralev's 'Authentic Leadership' workshops. We learned about the components that make a leader and different leadership styles, as well as which ones are most suited for each of us. In the first workshop, we were given a list of six famous leaders—Arianna Huffington, Bill Gates, George Steinbrenner, Walt Disney, Steve Jobs and Milton Hershey—and a short summary of their successes and failures. We were told to identify important traits that these leaders shared. 'They all failed terribly but didn't give up.' 'They all took a long time to reach success.' There were many similarities among these leaders. The one that stuck out the most to me was that they all initiated changes in the world around them. Even though many people were against them initially, they still believed in their own ideas for change and followed through with them, no matter how impossible they seemed. The people in the list were all entrepreneurs or innovators, and their perseverance had helped them in the entrepreneurial field. Still, I did not know how this particular characteristic tied in with leadership. It helped them become innovators, yes, but leaders?

From the second day of the camp, all fifty delegates took a 'Design Thinking' workshop, in which we learned skills for problem solving. Everyone was put into groups with people from all three countries; we were instructed to choose a problem that all three countries currently face and think of a solution to the problem. This solution had to be presented as a creative new business idea that could realistically be put into place. In order to do this, each group had to come up with a problem statement, the solution criteria, a prototype for the solution, and ways to implement that solution. On top of all of these things, each group had to prepare a PowerPoint presentation to introduce and explain their ideas to the Teaching Fellows, the staff and all the other participants. We had approximately a day and a half to complete all of this.

My group decided to focus on the problem of the high suicide rate among high school students in Japan, China and Korea, and we came up with two different solutions for this problem relatively quickly. After discussing the pros and cons of each solution, we chose one and started forming the problem statement, solution criteria, and prototype. However, at around 11 p.m. that night, one of my group members suddenly suggested that we stop and consider changing to the other solution. I was against this notion at first. We had worked for hours, focused on one solution, and he was suggesting that we change course now? In my mind, we just did not have time. Then the group member explained why he thought we should change the solution. In reality, the alternative solution made more sense and was more achievable for us. Still, at that moment my mind was so focused on finishing in time that I could not see the advantages of taking a different route and did not want to agree. I felt that he was somehow being selfish. When we took a vote, I voted to keep going with our original plan, but four people voted to change, so that was what we did.

The group member who had instigated the change apologized for causing such a disruption. What I realized later, though, was that he was being a leader as well as an innovator by initiating the change. By thinking of a different and better way to do things, and by assessing the advantages for the rest of the team as well, he created a change in the direction our group was moving. He inspired his teammates and helped us to see that the change would be beneficial. Was this not an act of leadership in itself?

Many of us are scared of change, myself included. A lot of people, whether they admit it or not, would rather be comfortable and stable than take risks. And a lot of people will always keep their eyes locked on the end result and not want to stray from the path, as I did when we worked on our project. Without that one person to initiate change, our group would have kept going in the exact same direction, not improving and perhaps even failing drastically. This is why a person who initiates change is called a 'leader'—they are 'leading' people onto a different path, whether it be good or bad.

The same can be said on a larger scale. One famous example of someone initiating change and becoming a leader is Mohandas Gandhi and his commitment to peaceful protests and civil disobedience in 20th century India. Word spread about Gandhi's movement because he was changing what no one else had changed so far. Many people were against the unfair treatment of native Indians at the time, but he was the first to fight it peaceably and to bring about change in this way, and his efforts resulted in supporters rallying around him, most memorably in the famous Salt March. In 1930, Gandhi and about eighty supporters began a 250-mile walk to collect salt from the sea as an act of peaceful protest against the salt tax. On the way, they were joined by tens of thousands of supporters, as more and more people realized what they were fighting for and were inspired to join in as well. My theory is that if someone initiates a change that interests other people, those people will naturally gravitate toward the person who first started the change. This is how many people who have not been chosen beforehand nevertheless become leaders.

But what can you do if you, like me, are afraid of change? One particular thought had been bothering me a lot lately, and getting rid of it during my five days at the TLS helped me make sense of my fear of change. I was worried that I wouldn't be able to settle on one professional path in the future. During our 'Career Mentoring' time on the fourth evening, everyone chose a different mentor depending on what kind of career they wanted to pursue in the future. Directly before this, the Teaching Fellows had given us tips for getting into universities in the U.S. One of their main tips was something I had heard several times before at other events: show your passion for something. By doing this, you prove that you are someone with enough interest in one field to study it throughout your time in college and beyond. Hearing this over and over again had always made me nervous, however, because I did not feel confident that I would be able to do it. In the past, I've developed interests in numerous different fields, only to lose interest later. As a result, I have always been terrified to think about the long life I have ahead of me. How can I focus on one thing for my entire life, when I get bored with everything I try in a matter of weeks? Thinking like this escalated my resentment of change and turning points.

I went to Mr. Tarnowski's group and listened to him talk about the variety of job experiences that he had had in the past. I was surprised to hear him say that he had taken time off of working at his stable job to work for a non-profit organization (NPO) in a different country and had decided to change jobs in this way several times. Nevertheless, at the same time, he continued to state the importance of being passionate enough about your job that you can do it for ten hours a day and still not get sick of it. This confused me; if he had lost interest in his previous jobs, didn't that mean he wasn't passionate about them? After speaking, Mr. Tarnowski went around the circle and asked each person what they were thinking about doing in the future, or if they had any questions. This is when I voiced my fear: would I really be able to stay passionate about the subject I studied in university for my entire life?

Mr. Tarnowski paused and then said, 'You don't have to have only one passion for your entire life. You can choose to change your job at any time when you're older, depending on your interests at the time.'

'But,' I replied, 'you said that we have to find something that we can do with passion for ten hours a day.'

That was when it finally clicked. It doesn't matter how long you stay passionate about one thing; you just need to pursue whatever you are passionate about at that moment. I had always been afraid of changing, assuming that it would be impossible or too risky. When I thought about it, however, I realized that plenty of successful people have done many different things. When Mr. Kim introduced himself, I was surprised to learn that he had worked for five different organizations throughout his life. I was also taken aback when Ms. Lee showed us a PowerPoint slide with the logos of the dozens of different companies and organizations she has worked for.

Previously, whenever I thought of passion, I always pictured an Olympic gymnast training from age three to win a gold medal twenty years later, or a musician devoting his whole life to playing one instrument. This was why I had thought that I too would have to find something I could be passionate about my whole life. I can't even count the times I have thought of myself as a failure because I cannot stick to one thing. The truth is, though, that passion isn't something that has to be displayed in only one field. You don't have to devote your time to one thing just to prove your commitment. There is nothing wrong with changing what you do according to the way your interests evolve.

Unfortunately, the current Japanese high school system does not do a good job reinforcing this point. At the age of fifteen or sixteen, all high school students in Japan have to make a life-changing decision: whether to pursue careers in the humanities or in the sciences. After that, every class you take is determined by this choice. It is not possible in most schools to change your mind once you have chosen a particular path. I have a number of friends who are already regretting the decision they made a few months ago, but the school will not allow them to change their curriculum, meaning that they will either have to teach themselves the other curriculum in their free time, or give up. It is very rare and difficult to transfer between these two curricula, and most people remain on the same track when they are choosing their majors in college, and eventually their jobs as well. This rigid system reinforces the idea that it is risky and unwise to change your trajectory in life once you've started on it. Could this also be the reason that many adults in Japan prefer to stay in one job for the rest of their lives, even if they are not particularly interested in it? This common habit among Japanese people could stem from the country's education system.

Steve Jobs once said, 'For the past thirty-three years, I have looked in the mirror every morning and asked myself, "If today were the last day of my life, would I want to do what I am about to do today?" And whenever the answer has been "No" for too many days in a row, I know I need to change something.' This spirit is extremely important when initiating drastic change. In places like Japan, people tend to pursue stable lifestyles and stay in one job even if they do not enjoy it, for the sake of stability and comfort. But these people must learn that it is often a better choice to pursue what is best at the moment, even if doing so means embracing the possibility of leading to a negative change.

And this goes for most things. In innovation, it is always important to remember that other options are available. Take Bill Gates, for example: before he created his first Microsoft product, he attempted to make a product that analyzed traffic tapes, which ended up being a disaster. However, he continued to explore new opportunities for useful inventions. By pinpointing the elements of the technology world that most needed to be changed and successfully creating something that actually did change those elements, he became a successful entrepreneur, leader and, eventually, billionaire.

What I learned in our 'Design Thinking' workshops at the TLS helped me to understand and embrace change. Ms. Lee emphasized the importance of pinpointing the part of the problem that we could actually change and of rephrasing it in a problem statement so that we could then think of ways to fix it. By framing the solution in this way, we could come up with our own original ideas. My group did not do well with our first solution, so we restated the problem statement and reframed the solution as well. It was difficult for me because I was so against change and worried about the consequences, but in the end, the exercise was an effective way for me to practice overcoming these transitions, whether in design thinking or in life in general.

Anybody can become a leader. As it says on the TLS bags that were handed out to each person at the beginning of the camp, 'Leadership starts with you.' There are so many aspects of leadership I did not know about prior to attending this camp. A leader can simply be the person who causes a change in a group. But I also discovered that 'change' is not always a simple concept. Deeply rooted thoughts often prevent us from seeking out change. Especially in Japan, the education system and our customs in general reinforce negative feelings toward change and spontaneity. It is crucial, therefore, that we work to get rid of this negativity, if we are to increase the number of our innovators and leaders and keep moving forward as a country.

I would like to call upon every single person reading this to reflect on their own lives and see if they have had any problems like the ones I have mentioned. I am sure that most, if not all, people have been in similar situations before. But I'm sure that you, like me, dream of being that one person who initiates a change that impacts people's lives, no matter how big or small that change is. If so, I urge you to focus on the phrase 'Don't settle.' If you see a problem in how something works, you can be the one to fix it. If you think that something could be made even better, you should feel free at least to attempt to put your ideas into motion. By doing this, we can bring many changes to our societies and also, as importantly, to our own lives. And at the same time, each and every one of us can become leaders and change makers.

To be effective leaders, however, it is important to embrace the value of change. Instead of thinking of change as something negative, as our schools and societies often teach us, we need to think of it in a completely new light. Working on our presentation for the Design Thinking workshops made me realize just how close-minded I could be when it came to this topic. As you can see from looking at examples of past leaders and change makers, initiating change is the only way we can ever move forward and improve. We should never be afraid of that process.

I am grateful that I had my eyes opened to the importance of change in many different situations. This experience has given me more confidence not only in leadership and innovation but also in my life as a whole.

| Chapter 17 |

My TLS Experience

Annie Dawon Lee

● ● ●

During the five-day TLS, I don't think there was a single day when Mr. Kim didn't remind us, 'Together, we can change.'

At the time, I simply took his word for it. I mean, a distinguished Harvard graduate telling me that we, as the future generation, can inspire change. So I believed him: perhaps we can make a change. And now, reflecting back on my experiences at this Summit, I can see that the five short days truly have made a significant impact on the way I now define leadership; they have made me reshape my own goals for the future.

Our first workshop, titled 'The Practice of Negotiation,' was run by Mr. Kim. As he eloquently explained to us the difference between distributive and integrative negotiation, I thought, 'I've negotiated before: distributive negotiating when I compromised on the price for a bag of peaches in the street markets, and integrative negotiating when I made an agreement with my mom to watch TV after finishing my homework.' So, when we practiced the first case study in pairs, I dove in and tried to get the best deal for myself. In the case study, I was Ryan Kim, an agent representing a band, and my task was to sign a contract with a recording company at the highest possible signing-on price for the band. It didn't take me long to end the negotiation with what I thought was a pretty good deal. Yet, as we shared the final price of negotiation that each pair had agreed on, I was surprised to realize that the price I had gotten was, in fact, on the lower end of the spectrum. As I tried to wrap my head around this strange result, I also carefully listened to Mr. Kim's explanation of the case and his introduction of new acronyms, such as BATNA (Best Alternative To a Negotiated Agreement) and ZOPA (Zone Of Possible Agreement).

On the next day, as we handled the second case study, I tried to apply my learning in practice. In my head, I had step-by-step procedures that I wanted to take during the negotiation. Although again I was a seller, selling my car for the highest possible price, this time I went into the negotiation with a set BATNA—the lowest price I was willing to accept for the car. I also remembered to listen carefully to figure out the highest possible price that the buyer was willing to pay. Through such practices, I realized that, without knowing it, I was becoming more mindful and strategic in my approach to the negotiation. Surprisingly, such tactics allowed me to end my negotiation with a good price, on the higher end of the spectrum.

Afterward, I wondered how the results of the two case studies could have been so different. In both cases, I had the same goal as the seller: to negotiate the highest possible price in the deal. Yet in these two, small exercises, I realized that my mindful approach—of strategically deciding either to talk or to listen first, and of setting the right mood for the conversation before beginning the negotiation—actually had an impact on the final results of the negotiation. I had learned a key lesson: my words and actions conveyed more meaning to those I interacted with than I had expected.

This realization was critical to my personal leadership development. It occurred to me that, as a leader, I could actually stir change in those around me through my words and actions. It made even more sense to me when I thought back to the times when people have said that great leaders are also great speakers. And Mr. Tarnowski's 'Leadership Communications' lecture proved to me why good communication skills are so critical in good leadership.

In his workshop, we learned the art of persuasion through the framework of Aristotle's three persuasive techniques: Logos, Ethos and Pathos. Logos is the use of logic and reason to convince the mind of the audience. Ethos is an ethical appeal and involves using credibility to help the audience better understand and trust the author's character. Finally, Pathos is an appeal to the emotions, often through stories and adhesion. Through a good speech—one that uses Aristotle's Ethos, Logos and Pathos framework—leaders are able to change the way people feel about a certain cause, provoke understanding and persuade their audiences to rethink their values.

In my opinion, Pathos was the most difficult to achieve, since it involved changing how others feel, and as we can see from any set of opposing political or religious parties, it is hard to get a group of people who disagree with you to understand your viewpoint. It requires placing yourself in the other person's shoes and strategically convincing them through their emotions. I felt particularly inspired to incorporate Pathos into my future speeches and wanted to practice this skill during Mr. Tarnowski's workshop.

We watched videos of speeches by both good and poor speakers to see how Aristotle's framework was used in real life. For the good speeches, we examined Malala Yousafzai's speech at the Youth Takeover of the United Nations and Donovan Livingston's Harvard graduation speech, and then we compared these two to Phil Davison's poorly delivered Republican candidate speech. I found that the great speeches elegantly incorporated Aristotle's three concepts, and this prompted me to ponder ways in which I myself could become a better speaker and leader, whether at school, in my community or in my future workplace.

Practicing these skills through the public speaking exercise in Mr. Tarnowski's workshop with students from China, Korea and Japan was a great privilege. There was one exercise in which everyone paired off and shared with their partner one national issue that worried them. This exercise got me thinking about what issue mattered most to me. An endless number of issues have affected me, including sexism, the stressful education system in Korea, the declining economy and Korea's historical conflicts with Japan and China. It was hard to choose only one. In the end, I decided to talk about the issue of air pollution and increasing yellow dust in Korea. I shared with my partner my concern that not only does the increasing air pollution negatively affect our health but it also has become an inconvenience in our everyday lives, by preventing many outdoor activities and forcing people to wear masks when the air is particularly bad. I spent most of my childhood outdoors in the playground, but now the increased air pollution is making many parents prevent their children from staying outside, which could lead to a lack of exercise and increased studying time for younger children.

In sharing my story of why this issue was important to me, I practiced using Pathos in my speech. After I had shared my concerns for two minutes, my partner gave a short reflection on it, saying that he now understood how this could be an issue. He also talked about how he too had spent much time on the playground as a child and how he would have been sad if he had been prevented from doing so and had been told to wear a mask simply when walking to and from school.

Then, in the next two minutes, my partner, who was from Japan, talked about how the low voting turnout, especially in the younger generation, was affecting the ideas supported by the government. Because the number of elderly in Japan has been increasing and a smaller number of younger people are getting involved in politics in Japan, traditional views are more frequently expressed in the government, which he believed was not reflective of the progressive ideals of the younger generation. While I was unsure about Korea's voting turnout, I knew that the increasing elderly population was also an issue in Korea. Our discussion made me reconsider what consequences a low voting turnout could have on the country's politics.

Through the sharing of our stories, we were able to confide our passions and worries in each other and, in return, empathize with our partner in the short five minutes that we had. Our words, creating understanding between us, also prompted us to consider and relate to new issues. The exercise helped me redefine leadership. To me, good leadership comes from more than just exercising power over a group of people. More importantly, it is about sharing stories, a cause and understanding with a group of people. With good communication skills, we can become better leaders and speakers, and thus unite a group of people to support the causes we care about.

Our words and actions, though they may feel unimportant at the time, can create ripple effects and change the way others feel and think. Often, I have felt that to be a leader and a true change maker in society, I would need to have a position in a place like the government or the United Nations; that we, as young teenagers, still had a long way to go before speaking out on troubling issues. However, Ms. Lee's workshop on 'Trilateral Design Thinking Simulation' showed me that we were in fact not too young to implement small changes in our community. During this workshop, Ms. Lee asked us, for our final project, to choose an issue that we cared about and then to devise a possible solution to this issue in small groups of about six students.

My group decided to focus on high school and college students lacking the time and opportunity to explore various careers, majors and personal interests. Due to the educational systems in China, Japan and Korea, in which students are taught core academic subjects not through real-life applications but through taking tests and studying in classrooms, we felt that many high school and college students do not deeply consider what careers will interest them. In fact, many end up choosing their majors according to their grades or how well certain jobs pay, rather than considering their own interests. We viewed this as a problem because if you do not consider your personal interests, it is easy to lose interest in what you are studying. Students no longer work for what truly excites them but for what they believe is the correct way of achieving economic and social success. We felt that this issue could lead to increased unhappiness in the workplace and a lack of efficiency in how people handle their daily tasks in their careers.

Ms. Lee helped us devise possible solutions that we thought could help solve this issue. It seemed daunting at first—we were only high school students ourselves. However, as she took us through a step-by-step process of finding the source of our problem and then devising a map to think about how our solutions could be implemented in the real world, we began to come up with more and more ideas about how our problem could be solved.

Ms. Lee introduced us to new and creative tactics that we could use in this brainstorming process; one strategy that stuck with me was using sticky notes to organize thoughts. While I had previously used sticky notes for short reminders or as additions to my notes when I ran out of paper space, Ms. Lee uses sticky notes because they are easy to see, move around and dispose of, unlike a sheet of paper or online documents. We first wrote down all of our thoughts on different colored sticky pads, with only one thought per sticky note, as she suggested. Then, one by one, we went around sharing our thoughts, and we realized that many of our solutions overlapped in one way or another. Because each of our thoughts was written on a single sticky note, it was easy for us to categorize our opinions and place our sticky notes together on a large piece of paper, about the size of four student desks.

After we did this several times, our group was able to come up with a solution that consolidated everyone's opinions. We decided that providing students with opportunities to participate in internship and shadowing programs at different workplaces could help them understand what skills are required of each job and show them how their interests could be applied in the real world. We also suggesting having career mentoring systems in schools that would prompt students to consider their personal interests before choosing their majors or jobs.

While it is true that our solution isn't perfect and is seemingly impossible for us, high school students, to put into action now, this exercise sparked my group's interest in this issue. We made a Facebook page and a group chat, where we occasionally talk about the possibility of this initiative. Although it seems unlikely to be implemented any time in the near future—especially since we are all currently busy studying—Ms. Lee fostered in us the belief that we can actually be agents of change if we put in the necessary time and effort.

We often hear about how young people got together to begin a start-up or how a college student is helping to find a cure for cancer. Whenever I heard about such people, I ask myself, 'How are these students making such large accomplishments at a young age?' What is important to keep in mind is that such seemingly large accomplishments all began from a small cause that sparked their interest individually. Then they followed their interest and either convinced a group to support their cause or found people who were willing to help them achieve their goals. They had the belief that their words and actions could lead to change, and thus they continued working.

All of these realizations in my short five days at the TLS have made me reshape my goals for the future. The five-day program made me understand that being a leader is not solely about what position you hold in the government, or what power you have. Instead, it is about taking the initiative to make a difference in the lives of the people around you through mindful words and actions. In order to do this, you need to practice good communication skills, find an issue that you want to work toward solving and begin to spark change in other people's lives. This has become my ultimate goal in life: to be an agent of change in the global community I live in.

During the program, when Mr. Tarnowski decided to stay behind one night to share his advice for career planning, or when Ms. Lee offered to share her personal college experiences, their words made an impact on the way I thought about applying to colleges and pursuing careers in different fields of studies. Mr. Tarnowski shared his experiences of working in the non-profit sector and being a Fulbright Scholar after he graduated. Thanks to his advice, I will be open-minded and will 'take the time to explore different career opportunities' when considering careers after graduation. As Mr. Tarnowski hinted, one of our interests may lead us to an unexpected career. This spring, when I begin choosing my final college this year, I will have Ms. Lee's experiences of attending a large urban school in mind. She shared with us her experiences of adjusting to a large school and how she actually ended up changing majors during her undergraduate years to follow her interest in international relations. I was able to relate with her struggle to balance her own academic wants with her parents' desires. When attending college next year, I will consider my own interests when choosing my major and will also take advantage of the opportunities provided at my school.

All the faculty at the TLS are change makers in one way or another. Their words and actions have truly made a difference to me, as well as to hundreds of other students. Whether you are curious about others' experiences at this program or are looking for ways to improve your own leadership skills, I suggest that you summon the courage to admit that you will be, if you are not already, a leader for your community. Your words and actions will have an impact on those around you, but how you use your abilities depends solely on you. Thus, I encourage you to begin finding issues that you care about, depending on your interests and experiences. Don't be afraid of what is preventing you from reaching a goal but focus instead on the possibilities of your goal. Be mindful of how you say things and of what has caused you to act in a certain way because your seemingly unimportant words and actions can cause a ripple effect and change how others navigate their paths. Keep asking questions about your own actions and look for ways to improve your communication skills by sharing your opinions with others.

These are some ways in which we can improve our leadership and communication skills. Through my reflections on my personal leadership development at the TLS, I hope I have made you rethink what leadership means to you and how you plan to practice leadership skills in your own community. While there is no one definition of being a good leader, I think that one must keep in mind that leadership is about serving others and not about serving oneself. I have no doubt that with these important qualities in mind, we truly can make positive change.

| Chapter 18 |

Breaking Out of My Shell

Shiina Yuri

● ● ●

Arriving at Incheon Airport, my heart was filled with anxiety about the upcoming five-day TLS, facilitated by Teaching Fellows from Harvard University. In this program, all the delegates—high school students from Korea, China and Japan—would have the opportunity to take two workshop series on the themes of leadership and innovation. When I first heard about the program, it really attracted me, since I've long wanted to study at Harvard University. Also, my dream is to become the Prime Minister of Japan, so I saw this program as a chance for me to gain leadership experiences and skills.

Though I was excited to have been chosen as a delegate, however, I gradually grew worried about my ability to take part in the program. I was born and brought up in Japan, and my greatest concern was whether or not I could understand and make myself understood in English. Also, while I had experience working as a leader in school, I still did not know how to lead a group. These concerns kept me awake almost all night the day before I left Japan.

Throughout the first and second day of the TLS, I remained in my shell. I couldn't shout out when Ms. Lee, a passionate and lovely teacher, asked us to do so during games, and I couldn't raise my hand when Mr. Kim asked, 'Any volunteers?' Fortunately, I was able to understand the lectures and make myself understood in English. As a result, I soon realized that my lack of confidence came not from my clumsy English but from my passive and negative behavior. At this Summit, it didn't matter whether your English was fluent or not; what mattered was how actively you were involved in the discussions, lectures, presentations and other activities. Seeing other delegates having animated discussions, I wanted to get involved as well—I was eager to improve, learn and grow, as well as gain confidence. But I didn't know how to do it.

Then, when I was feeling most dejected at my weakness, the first miracle happened: I got to know my roommate, Jiho, a Korean girl who was younger than I am. She was so positive and confident in herself that she was able to ask questions and convey her ideas actively during classes, and she had a wide-ranging perspective on trilateral relationships and educational matters in the three countries. I held her in high esteem for her ambitions and confidence. I also felt very comfortable with her, since she loved Japan. She explained that she had planned to visit Japan several years ago, but couldn't because of the huge earthquake, and she also spoke about how deeply she sympathized with the earthquake's victims. She gave me an impressive speech about how strongly she wanted to try Japanese ramen. Thanks to her friendliness, we soon became good friends, staying up late at night and talking about our school days and our dreams.

During our conversations, I asked her how she had built her confidence. She answered, 'Whenever I get the chance to speak in public or to lead a group, I make use of that opportunity. I raise my hand every time I have ideas or questions. Through such experiences, I have naturally come to feel less worried in front of other people.' Inspired by her example, I made up my mind to make the most of the opportunities at the TLS; to raise my hand when teachers asked us to speak out; and to be a volunteer. The next day, I tried to express my opinion and ask as many questions as possible. In Mr. Kim's negotiation class, though I had concerns about my English, my partner, Taturo, and I raised our hands to perform a negotiation demonstration. My heart was leaping into my mouth, but when I heard everyone's applause, I was filled with a sense of achievement. I felt I became a little stronger.

Thus, my late night conversations with Jiho served as an impetus for me to become an active participant. Through my conversations with her and with other friends from China and Korea, I came to be confident and take responsibility as a delegate from Japan. Because my roommate was such a wonderful person, my first impression of Korea was that it was a very friendly country. There are many problems between Korea and Japan, but my feelings were formed by my conversations with Jiho. Pro-Japanese, warm-hearted, hardworking, polite… Perhaps these do not apply to all Korean people, but this was my impression of the country.

Then I thought about myself. My new Chinese and Korean friends might be seeing Japan through me, and I felt a new responsibility to represent Japan well. This awareness helped me gain confidence and become more actively involved in the program. I think that my friends, whatever country they were from, felt the same awareness, and I believe that meeting friends who are acting as delegates from their countries is a wonderful experience and helps you to become more independent and confident.

Though I had built some confidence, I was still worried about my ability to lead a group. However, Mr. Lim's workshop, '21st Century Skills and Attributes,' helped me gain insights into adaptive leadership. I learned several key points. First, you should manage your emotions authentically: anticipate how you will feel in a given situation and prepare for it; pay attention to the way you would naturally act in that situation; and, when surprised, remember your moral compass. Second, you should avoid your natural egocentric bias. Begin with figuring out the values that are important to you. Let others speak first, and listen to their words, paying attention to facial expressions and body languages. When probing, make sure you ask the right questions to find out what other people are thinking. It's not what you say that matters, it's what they hear. Also, you cannot be too empathetic when speaking. Third, you shouldn't behave defensively. Protecting yourself is natural, and you will struggle with this, but you have to be confident in yourself. Be proactive in asking for constructive feedback from the people around you. For example, you could ask a question starting, 'How can I be a better…?' Fourth, you should know how to build trust with the people around you. Choose partners well and accept some vulnerability. Fifth, learn what motivates others. It is usually based on values and identities. When explaining this part, Mr. Lim mentioned a famous baseball manager who worked for the Yankees. His motivation was not money but pride. From this example, we learned that it is not always easy to understand what motivates others, but at the same time we understood that this is an important part of uniting people in their pursuit of a common goal.

After the workshop, I asked Mr. Lim for tips on how to keep a good balance between listening to others and conveying my own opinions. I told him about my failure when I had led a group at school. Last year, my class had to decide what event to run for our school festival. Two ideas came up: making a big maze or performing a play. We had ten executive committee members, and I was the leader of the group. Eight members supported the idea of performing a play. The vice-leader and I wanted to opposed them; we thought that since only a small number of people would be responsible for writing the script and making the props, it would be a confusing and imbalanced project. However, fearing that expressing disagreement as a leader might cause disruption and worrying that I would be seen as a dictator, I did not express my thoughts and gave in to the proponents of the play without arguing. I knew that suppressing my own opinion and giving in to others was not what 'leadership' encompasses, but I was too worried that I would be an autocratic person, and that there would be a mood of dissent among the team members, to speak up.

In Mr. Lim's answer to my question, four points impressed me. First, an important thing when working as a leader is to understand each group member's background, values, customs, beliefs and way of thinking. As he had said before, asking questions and knowing how your teammates are motivated can help you understand their hidden perspectives and how they are looking at the matter at hand. This will make it easier to lead a group without bad feelings, even if different ideas are raised. It is also important in making progress as a whole team. Second, finding allies can be a powerful strategy. This is not a formal relationship but an informal one. The more people agree with you, the more easily you can lead your group. You can find allies by doing what others want you to do, giving something to them or doing them a favor. Third, Mr. Lim told me about the 'Dance Floor and Balcony' idea, which he had also referred to in his workshop. This concept suggests that in a confused situation—for example, on a dance floor—it is important to step away 'onto the balcony' in order to understand the situation from a different angle. Mr. Lim said that the concept holds true when leading a group. In a tense situation, when some members oppose others and the team doesn't seem to be progressing, it is important to step back and remind people of their main purpose. Reminding your members of their central purpose can help prevent the team from falling into disarray. Fourth, he told me that a certain extent of disequilibrium is necessary for a group to make progress. A demanding and forceful leader can be a catalyst for others to progress, but a group with a leader who compromises too much will not be able move forward. Mr. Lim told me that I must learn to be comfortable with uncertainty and tension.

I wanted to know more about managing my emotions, so Mr. Lim introduced me to Mr. Tarnowski, a Harvard Teaching Fellow, during lunch time. Mr. Tarnowski told me that gaining experience can help me get used to new situations, and that I shouldn't worry about failure. What made me feel most relieved was that he told me even a great leader like Barack Obama will inevitably make numerous mistakes and go through difficult times. Mr. Tarnowski recommended that I read the life stories of great people so that I can learn from their experiences. He also said that self-examination is important as a leader. For example, I should always ask myself, 'Am I acting as a dictator or a weak leader?' and reflect on my own behavior. He told me it is equally useful to ask others for feedback. After our talk, I made up my mind to make the most of every chance I could get during the program. Thanks to these wonderful Teaching Fellows, I was ready to become a stronger person. This was the second miracle that happened to me at the TLS.

Putting what I had learned into practice, I decided to make a speech in front of all the delegates on the last day of the program. The speech would be based on what I learned in Mr. Tarnowski's 'Authentic Leadership' class. In the beginning, he talked about Public Narrative. This is the leadership practice of translating values into action; it combines the stories of 'self,' of 'us,' and of 'now.' There is leadership in 'self,' shared values and experiences in 'us,' and strategy and action in 'now.' But each part must relate to the others. You have to be prepared, when making a speech, for the question, 'So what?' There must also be a sense of urgency. We have to be ready to answer the question, 'Why now?' or 'Why can't we do it twenty years from now?' Lastly, you must think about the purpose of what you are saying. Mr. Tarnowski explained three rules about Public Narrative. First, as a leader, you should accept your responsibility to speak up for those who do not have the same opportunities. Second, each of us has a compelling story to tell. Pain can lead you to feel desire and drive, and it can enable you to think about the changes you want to make. The same can be said of hope, which can remind you of the belief that we can change, and you can then focus your attention on the necessity of change. Third, public narratives are based on action; they are made up of knowledge in our heads and feelings in our hearts. To help explain this concept, Mr. Tarnowski described Aristotle's framework for an impressive speech: Ethos, Pathos and Logos. Ethos is similar to 'ethics.' In your speech, you have to show your audience that you are a credible person. Pathos is similar to 'empathy.' If you can make your audience feel what you feel, you can make a stronger impression on them. Logos is of course about 'logic.' Using statistics, numbers or other kinds of data that strengthen your explanations will make your opinion more convincing. In addition to all that, I learned some performance techniques to make my speech even more powerful, including gestures, eye contact, the effective use of pauses and more.

After learning about the various characteristics of a good speech, we watched a video of a famous speech—Barack Obama's keynote address, made when he was an Illinois State Senator, on July 27, 2004, at the Democratic National Convention in Boston, Massachusetts. Though I had heard his speech before (I have a recording of it at home), this was the first time I had listened to it from an analytical point of view. I was surprised to recognize that Obama effectively used Ethos, Pathos and Logos. I could clearly identify the different aspects in his speech, and I could also understand why so many people have said that this speech is first class. Impressed by both Mr. Tarnowski's lecture and Obama's speech, I too wanted to give a powerful oration that would impress everyone in the hall. The speech I was going to make would be a description of the progress I had made at the TLS, based on what I had learned in Mr. Tarnowski's class. I wanted to demonstrate that I had become a stronger person and gained confidence through the Summit. With considerable spirit, I started to think about what I wanted to convey to my audience.

On the third night of the Summit, a Japanese delegate, Midori, came to my room. We stayed up all night (it was the first time I had ever done that!) and talked about our ambitions, our interest in volunteer activities, and our passion for sports. Midori had a clear vision about her future, and she had previously been involved in many projects and academic papers. She had a lot of experience, and I felt great respect for her. But what made me comfortable spending time with her was that we could talk not only about academic matters but also about other things, like school events. Thanks to my conversations with Midori, I managed to select a theme for my speech. It would be about my passion for law and my responsibility to speak out for those who are voiceless. The day before we had to give our speeches, I stayed up late again (I was awake for forty-four consecutive hours!), and though I was really sleepy, I had a lot of fun preparing what I was going to say. I was excited to have such a big opportunity for me to break out of my shell.

On the last day, we first gave our group presentations. Our team did a great job, thanks to Ms. Lee's workshop; we had learned how to think creatively, and how to cooperate well with each other. By working with my group mates, I realized that interacting with people from other cultures means a lot for young people. I have two reasons for this. First, we can share each country's problems and think creatively about them. Since we are young and have less knowledge than adults, we sometimes have unrealistic views and ideas about serious problems, but I think this actually helps a lot. We are still students now, without the power to make rules or new systems, but when we grow up, we will surely become people who can change the world. Sharing problems and ideas while young can contribute to our thinking processes when we are older. For instance, at this conference, I recognized for the first time that the Korean suicide rate is very high. Korean students, including friends I met in the program, study all day and are under considerable stress. When discussing this matter, I was shocked to hear that Korean students would not be surprised to hear that someone they know had committed suicide. I strongly felt that I wanted to change this situation. In my group, our main discussion theme was 'How do we help high school students who are stressed out but don't have chances to speak out?' We created a program called 'Schooltopia,' which would run conferences for students, parents and teachers, as well as organizing polls to help students. Our presentation was so successful that we got compliments from the Teaching Fellows. And in addition to our success, I noticed an important thing: I was naïve. Though I read every page of the newspapers every day, and carefully read *TIME* magazine and check *BBC News* online, I have more and more things to learn. I have once read that environment surrounding Korean students are miserable, but that was just letters on paper. In this program, it was the first time for me to hear their real voices. By communicating with foreign friends, I could broaden my view, which is indispensable for being active worldwide.

The second reason is that making friends with delegates from other countries can help us build strong relationships for the future. Since we are from different countries and have big ambitions and high motivations, our friendship will help us cooperate and change the world in the near future. I think it was a great experience for me to meet people from different parts of Asia, since we all have the same goal: the development of Asia.

Finally, we moved on to the individual speeches. Besides me, there were five students who were going to give their speeches. I was the second person to speak. The person before me gave a powerful talk about trilateral relationships, and the hall broke out into applause. Before I knew it, it was my turn to go up. I took a deep breath and walked to the center of the stage. As I looked over the full hall, I felt surprisingly comfortable in the midst of the tense situation. All the Teaching Fellows were looking at me, waiting for my speech, but since I had prepared and practiced a lot for it, I had no worries about my performance. In my speech, I could fully express my thoughts. And, to my great joy, my speech was received with cheers! Mr. Tarnowski even approached me afterward and told me that my speech had been wonderful.

After the last speaker ended his speech, I high-fived all the other speakers. I was really excited to be a stronger person. I hadn't expected that I could change so much in such a short span of time. I was moved to tears. I really could break out of my shell!

At the closing ceremony, Mr. Kim asked some of us to share our feelings and experiences. Midori looked at me. Her eyes were saying that I should raise my hand. If I were the person that I had been five days before, I would have shrunk back and stayed in my seat. But thanks to the five days of the TLS program, I had gained confidence. I made use of that chance and walked toward the stage.

When I got back to my high school, my first chance to practice what I had learned at the program was during our sports festival. I decided to take part by being the leader of the cheerleading team. My job was to lead the cheering during the events, which is usually considered to be one of the hardest tasks. I shouted, waved big flags and beat a drum. I was absorbed in leading all the other members, but I didn't forget to observe my own behavior objectively: 'Am I a reliable leader, who has leadership but is not too demanding? Am I motivating others to take part in the cheering more actively?' I also asked my friends and teachers for feedback. Though I tried to think about my own performance as much as possible, it turned out that there were a lot of things I wasn't taking into consideration. 'Did you notice that quite a few bored students were lying behind the cheering bench?' my teachers said. 'Encourage them to join us!' 'Your explanation is not so easy to understand,' my friends told me. 'Can you speak a little slower?' During the festival, I listened to this kind of advice from my teammates and tried to apply it to my leadership style. This was what I couldn't do before the TLS and what I've learned from it. As a result of what I learned, my team won the championship for the cheerleading section!

This sports festival was a big success for me because I could put into practice what I learned during the TLS; I could see that what I'd gained actually worked. And this experience as a leader strengthened my confidence even more. Through the TLS, I experienced several miracles that greatly changed me, especially meeting Jiho, Midori, Mr. Lim, Mr. Tarnowski and all the wonderful delegates and Teaching Fellows. And these wonderful encounters weren't just miracles; they were a direct result of participating in the program. After the Summit, I can definitely say that I am not the person I used to be. I would like to express my deepest gratitude to Mr. Kim for being in charge of the event, which helped pave the path for my future. I will treasure my lifelong connections with the lovely Fellows and make use of every chance to gain greater confidence in myself.

| Chapter 19 |

A Memorable Experience

Jiho Hwang

● ● ●

"That's not the right way. Why would you solve it like that anyway? Please go back to your seat."

I was just back from the U.S. when this happened. I really love speaking out and sharing my own opinions, so when our math teacher asked someone to come up and show how to solve a math problem, I raised my hand, as I always have. But that was what my math teacher said after I presented to the class. Although I had solved the problem, it was not what she wanted. She wanted the 'textbook' way of solving the problem, not something innovative from a fifteen-year-old in her class.

This is a normal scene in Korea and elsewhere in Asia. I believe people of other nations know about the education system here and the predicament of the students. Especially in Korea, though some schools are improving, most schools limit the students' ability to think creatively, which leads to an increase in the number of 'mechanical Asians,' Asians who can't come up with their own unique ideas. This is also causing the minority who have different ideas to be afraid to speak up, for fear of getting unwelcome attention. Because of this background, teachers who have standardized minds correct students, just as my teacher corrected me. Gradually, that day, I began to feel uncomfortable and embarrassed, as the other students shook their heads at me, telling me to go sit down.

The TLS was a magical opportunity for me to change my current self. I had a chance to go when my English teacher, knowing my passion for international relations, introduced me to the program. The first time I heard the name of the camp, my heart started to pound with excitement; the word trilateral gave me a feeling that God had given me a chance to overcome my fears by meeting new people. And my feelings about the TLS were absolutely correct.

The classes wouldn't have been complete without my outstanding fellow delegates. They had tons of abilities and potential. One of the delegates had already written a chapter of a professional book and met the Bhutanese king to have deep conversations with him, despite her young age. Another delegate, the president of the Youth Union of Politics and Diplomacy (YUPAD), has accomplished a lot to unite youth in diplomacy, although he's only in the second year of high school. Many delegates were already leaders in their schools or places of work, and I learned so many things from them. But what surprised me most was that all of us learned and changed during the sessions and activities of the TLS.

The classes were excellent and had a great impact on my views of life, goals, and the world. One that inspired me greatly was Ms. Lee's 'Creative Thinking' workshop. When I first looked at the name of the class, I didn't feel so excited, to be honest. To think creatively was something I'd always wanted to do, but based on the experiences I'd had in the past, I thought of myself as a person empty of creativity. When I was in the third grade, I participated in a creative thinking contest. I was supposed to describe and make a house with given materials. As soon as the timer started, I tried to think faster than the other participants, but soon I was panicking because I had no idea how to build creative things with my hands. Actually, I did have ideas, but I thought they were either too common or too weird to be introduced in a school contest. So for about one hour I sat there, trying to think creatively while others were praised for being creative thinkers. After the contest was over, all I had was embarrassment and a paper filled with scribbles. Since then, I had thought I wasn't born with an ability to think creatively, not knowing that this sort of thinking is not a God-given talent. Therefore, without any expectations of being able to change myself, I entered the first session of the workshop.

The first thing Ms. Lee did was put people in groups. After that, she told us how the exercise was going to work and then told us the story of a boy called Gavin, who was in the youth national soccer team because he was so talented at the sport. However, because of an unexpected car accident, he lost his sight, which was essential for his future as a sports player. Ms. Lee told us to imagine ourselves as his teachers, realizing that Gavin, at all times, is depressed and defensive. Yet he still shows some interest in soccer, moving around with a soccer ball in his hands. While everyone listened attentively to this poor boy's story, Ms. Lee threw us a question: 'Can Gavin still play soccer, without his eyesight?' I mouthed 'no' as a response, thinking that if something like this were introduced in a TV show, they would probably focus on some way to make him see again normally. Plus, I thought about how it would hurt his family, seeing him get stressed out and hate the fact that he might have ended up playing soccer under different circumstances. But Ms. Lee wanted us to find a way for Gavin to play soccer, even without his eyesight! I was impressed by this and started to think deeply, only to end up with more hesitation than before. After a few seconds, Ms. Lee asked us to write down first what we think would be a problem when Gavin played soccer and then solutions to those problems. Finally, she told us to share our ideas with our groups and come to a conclusion.

My group talked with each other and discovered that we had similar answers. Gavin wouldn't be able to communicate with his teammates and see where all the other players were. Our solution was to make a ball that has bells in it, putting extra layer of soft mats on the ground for him to have a lower risk of injury, and making a rule that all players in the field have to wear high-tech headsets to communicate with each other and with Gavin. Eventually, each group wrote out their solutions on a paper attached to the wall. Ms. Lee looked through them and showed us two groups' solutions, which used more scientific technology than others. We were awed by their creativity until she asked us if these were the best solutions we could have come up with, considering the financial limitations and Gavin's main problem. The moment she said it, I realized that I and the others had focused too much on making his eyes work again, the way I had thought about at the beginning. 'Why was his eyesight so important anyway?' I thought.

After this, Ms. Lee told us to go back to our seats and showed us a video of blind soccer in Brazil. The players used a ball with bells inside, and they all wore blindfolds except the goalkeepers. Those rules were enough to get the game going. Their coach said people often wonder if they are really blind because they play so well, communicating and leading each other in every game they play. After watching the video, I was impressed by the rules and technologies that kept the game going, but what impressed me even more was how the blind soccer team had put so much effort into their achievements and were grateful for their lives despite their uncomfortable situation. Some were born blind, but others had become blind because of tragic accidents, just like Gavin. But they didn't feel depressed. During an interview, Dudu, one of the blind players, said that for him being blind didn't matter so much. He wanted to live like this for the rest of his life because God had made him blind. I was so ashamed, recalling the many moments when I had blamed others for failures in my life. Because of their teamwork and perspective on life, they managed to change their "tragic" life to a grateful one. Those people in Brazil took on their challenge with gratitude and resourcefulness. And the tools they used were not high-tech like the solutions that we had thought of. It didn't require much for Gavin to play soccer and communicate with his teammates. I realized then that the fact that it would be hard for Gavin to play football wasn't the real problem. I had focused on trying to make Gavin's eyes work like normal people's and come up with a headset that let him visualize the field and walkie talkies to help him hear what everyone else was doing; we had even thought of eye transplant surgery. But, all the time, the real problem was how to change the rules of the game and the stereotypes that we and the world have about people like him.

By creative thinking, we can change our perspective on the world. Someday, maybe tomorrow or today, you will face a problem. To solve it creatively, your perspective needs to be different from others' viewpoints. Fixing a situation so that it goes back to what it used to be may not always be the best or the right way of solving it. There are lots of Gavins out there, and to solve their problems, we must use creative thinking. The more you think creatively, the better you will be as a leader, because creativity is a quality all leaders should have. Leaders are creative thinkers who change the world step by step. The sessions with Ms. Lee taught me lots of lessons like this.

My thoughts matured in Ms. Lee's sessions, but I still felt a discomfort in my heart because before participating in the camp, I had decided on two things that I wanted to accomplish: experiencing real change in myself, and learning from the experience. When it came to my presentation skills, I didn't want to wait long for this change, but I still wasn't able to overcome my fears. So I became more and more eager to change. Finally, on the last day of the camp, I did manage to change my behavior and overcome my fears.

When we arrived at the camp for the first time and were introduced to the Teaching Fellows, I knew from their speeches that they would be different from most teachers in Korea. However, I was afraid to speak to them because all of the Fellows not only had a degree from Harvard, but had also done things to change the world. What they had done seemed like climbing Mt. Everest to me. So, feeling this distance from them, I was nervous just thinking about talking to them; I could imagine them questioning what I said. But my predictions were all wrong. Things started to change when Mr. Kim, in his negotiation class, asked one student to come to the front and act out a negotiation with him. As I had already seen other delegates speak up actively, I expected another person to raise his or her hand. But, unexpectedly, there was a long and awkward silence in the class. It got so long that I started feeling annoyed that nobody was raising their hands. Soon, I was desperately wishing for somebody to end the silence.

Then, I slowly rethought Mr. Kim's question. A voice in my heart began to shout, 'Why is it so hard to answer? You know how to answer. Give it a try.' And, suddenly, I felt that his question was directed at me. I had to take action to break away from the fears that I had developed over the years. This was the perfect opportunity to show myself who I really was. At last, I gathered every bit of courage in me, raised my hand, and acted out the negotiation. And it was a success! The feeling of triumph overwhelmed me. To be honest, the negotiation was awkward, and, thanks to my poor negotiation skills, it wasn't the best negotiation the class could have seen. But, nevertheless, I was so happy and grateful that I had actually volunteered to present in front of the class and our mentors. Moreover, in the middle of the role-play, Mr. Kim asked the other delegates what should be fixed, and they gave me some feedback. And this time it was not criticism from a teacher forcing ideals on me but students offering a variety of answers. I felt happy to have had a chance to present in front of the class again, but what I was happiest about was that the other delegates didn't have a 'wrong answer' look on their faces, even when they were correcting me. The supportive atmosphere gave me tons of courage and inspired me to participate with a greater passion in other activities. I was so happy that I could share my opinions freely, even though they weren't always the best answers to the questions.

After gaining the courage to accomplish the tasks I set for myself, I decided to speak up and share my worries about my career and the capacities I would need to acquire in order to do what I wanted in life. The other delegates, I could see, had a broad view of the future, and I wanted to know what had given them that view and how they had accomplished such things in their lives. Countless factors helped me to learn more, but, especially, I noticed that my point of view on life was too narrow while listening to Mr. Lim's story in the mentoring session. I chose to go to his session, because, when he had given his initial speech, he had told us that he had worked in many different areas. I wanted to learn more about the experience of working in different environments, countries, and places, and in the mentoring session I said to him, 'Mr. Lim, I'm worried. In Korea, students have to fill out a lot of documents at the end of each semester, and this year I have to write down what I want to be in the future. But I just don't know what I'm going to be.' Actually, I wasn't worried just because of a blank space on my document. I believed then that a dream for the future had to be a specific plan, and that you have to start making it come true in your teens. So I told Mr. Lim about my deepest concerns, curious to hear his answers.

Mr. Lim told me about a person he knows who had a great passion for working in science but ended up choosing a different major because he wanted to make people admire his parents for having a son who had majored in medicine at Stanford. Still, he kept chasing his dream, and one day, he started making a new kind of incubator for African babies who die just because there isn't enough money to buy incubators. He sold each of his new incubators for only US$25, which is less than 0.1 percent of the cost of incubators in the U.S.

Later, he became the CEO of his own incubator company. I was awed by his great accomplishment, and then Mr. Lim threw me a question: 'Had he been preparing since his youth for his life to be like this?' He waited, then continued, 'See, like him, most people don't know exactly what they will do in their lives. But eventually, if you follow your interests, you will discover that you are at the point you have always admired and wanted.'

What Mr. Lim said woke me up to reality. I used to be a person who dreamed of diving into the world and being a leader promoting peace between all countries. Really, though, I was a person locked in other people's belief that all things need to be planned out and expected. Therefore, I was constantly afraid that I wasn't prepared, and that fear changed me into a person who was afraid of speaking up.

Before the TLS, I was called the leader of my class or the class representative many times, but I always felt as if I were just the class 'servant.' I couldn't understand the classmates who relied on me and expected me to make the class better, without actually caring themselves. Also, I felt as if I didn't have real leadership, since all I was doing was being quick-witted, and I struggled to have courage even when simply asking the other students to be quiet. Now I realized what I was truly lacking. I needed to think more about why they relied on me. They had trusted me as a leader, a helper, and problem solver, but I had misunderstood this trust and ended up thinking that I was some kind of slave. Finally, today, I have realized that I can be a real leader by building meaningful trust with people around me and using my ability to gather people together. The truth is, I have never lacked leadership. It was just hidden inside of me, ready to be revealed. All I needed were opportunities to find my passion within me and to follow it.

So, after the TLS, I searched for those opportunities, hoping for a great change in me. And, thankfully, Shikoh, Kaya, Eunjin, Jimmy and Joseph gave me a wonderful opportunity to join the program they organized. I was very surprised to learn that this program is about improving relationships between Japan and Korea, which is what I too had dreamed of doing. We often meet together to discuss our ideas, and through this process, gradually, I am getting my passions, dreams and eagerness back. And as I retrieve all of these lost things of mine, I have recognized that my question to Mr. Lim was unwise. Why should we have to write down what we want to be in the future on a document, when we don't know what will happen in our lives anyway? I wish I could retrieve all those hours of worrying about what I needed to put in the document. Having specific plans can be important, but who really knows what will happen in the future? Having realized this, I feel as if I already have the potential to fulfil my dream of bringing real change to the world and promoting peace in Asia. I am confident now that I will be a true leader among others.

I want to thank CALI for this amazing experience. No other program has ever given me so many essential life lessons, so many debating and negotiating skills, and, most of all, so many true friendships. Also, I want to thank the staff from the three countries for helping us out and advising us to nurture our leadership qualities in the future. Finally, thanks to the delegates who allowed me to learn so much by sharing their unique experiences and by talking with me in the evenings about ways to improve the trilateral relationship.

| Chapter 20 |

An Enriching Learning Experience

Alex Wookyung Lee

● ● ●

I am Korean. You are Japanese.
I am Korean. You are Chinese.
I am Korean, and you can be anything.

Lesson 1: Respect Diversity

To those who are concerned about their ethnic identity, to those who are worried about being away from their country, and to those who are having a hard time using only one language, I want to tell you it's perfectly fine.

In 2011, in my sixth year in school, I had a hard time using only Korean while having conversations with Koreans. Although I had never stayed outside of Korea over twenty-one days, English felt more natural to me. Apart from my normal school friends, I was bilingual. Back then I had no clue that being bilingual was a blessing; instead I dreaded going to school because my friends would mock my clumsy use of Korean.

In 2013, in my eighth year in school, I was given a chance to study in New Zealand for three weeks. I was still using both English and Korean while talking to Koreans, and scolding myself for doing so. My trip to New Zealand changed me completely. I was brainwashed (in a good way). The friends and families I met during my stay in New Zealand were also bilingual—differently from me, since they spoke English and Filipino, but still, the fact that we were all bilingual didn't change. They had no trouble communicating because all of them were able to speak both languages. Also, when a Filipino was talking to a non-Filipino, nobody thought it was strange to use both languages at once. Being bilingual was treated with respect. In that atmosphere, I learned that it was not unusual or weird to use more than one language in conversations. It wasn't the way many others conversed, but it was okay. Nobody stared or mocked.

In the TLS, the most precious lessons I learned were from the lectures but also from the people. Diversity and individuality are the two things I most respect, and everybody seemed to respect each other at the Summit without trying to change one another. Knowing that the TLS was for only three countries—China, Japan and Korea—it came as a shock to meet so many people from diverse backgrounds. Most of the students were not entirely Korean, Japanese or Chinese; most of them had lived half their lives in foreign countries or had experiences staying outside their countries. The same was true of the lecturers: one, for example, was from Macedonia. In the past he was a Minister of Education in Macedonia, and now he is staying in Korea teaching leadership, as well as studying in the U.S. and the U.K. And he's just one of numerous examples.

At the TLS, I was able to spend time with other Koreans, conversing in both Korean and English. Speaking English to other Koreans felt wonderful, since it was torturous to restrain myself from using English during my life in Korea. Witnessing the same phenomenon being experienced by students of other nations—for instance, Japanese people speaking Japanese and English to one another—I felt a strong urge to cry with tears of joy. All my life I had been accused of my strangeness for being bilingual, enjoying speaking up in front of people, wanting to change what's ugly in the system, etc. But the people I met at the TLS didn't seem to consider these things as a problem. Encountering so many people from various environments told me that I was not alone. Diversity and individuality were highly regarded at the TLS. I had finally found a place where I can be myself, without any fingers pointed at me for doing so.

The main ideas I encountered at the TLS were as follows: (1) Be proud of your so-called abnormality. (2) Those who wish to get respect from others should respect others as well. (3) Consider people's diversity a gift. (4) Acknowledge that the experiences people have outside their homes are precious. And (5) Start learning from people who are different from you because that's the only way you can get any closer to richness in life.

Lesson 2: Stop Comparing People

I have often explained myself as being 'bias-free' because the society I live in, Korea, is full of stereotypes: 'Boys are better than girls at everything,' 'Children should be excluded from decision making,'

'Students with low grades must be terrible at everything,' 'Studying is the most important thing in life.' I had no interest in following these biases, which I thought automatically gave me the title of a bias-free person. However, I realized during the TLS that I wasn't 100 percent free from biases.

There were times when I missed my society, and that was because, back where I come from, people treated me as if I were the special one. All the people at the TLS were unique in their own individual way, and as a result, I felt myself blending in with others, which had never happened in my whole life. Nevertheless, I acknowledged, in the end, that I wasn't truly blending in, nor did anybody. Feeling hot with embarrassment that I had even considered such a concept as 'blending,' it suddenly hit me: everyone has a purpose, and so did I. It's impossible to blend in, do nothing and stay normal if there's any ability inside you.

Leaders are important in group work. Since I have almost only played the role of the leader, I lack experience in suggesting ideas to and getting direction from a leader, though, growing up, I always praised group members for supporting their leader, which requires great patience and wisdom. In the TLS I didn't lead the team. We all led the team. Nobody volunteered to act like a leader. Sometimes I suggested an idea, and sometimes I didn't—and that, as I say, is perfectly okay. There was no need to feel useless, unwanted and left out when there were no ideas to share because nobody is useless. No instructor demanded a leader from each group, which made everybody participate without waiting for the leader to do his or her job. It was a flawless choice, and it worked perfectly for the students at the TLS.

The experience served as an impetus that pushed me to work hard.

Also, most importantly, it made me realize that I wasn't free from biases. I still had a huge bias eating away at my insides. It was foolish of me to sort people according to their capability and skills, which cannot always be shown externally. One person can be a leader while another is an outsider who does his or her job silently but with great excellence, which makes him always wanted by other people. In short, a person's capability should not be judged by one short glimpse.

Lesson 3: Be Passionate

'If you're passionate about soccer, you can't get enough of it—you've got soccer pennants plastered on your walls, your TV is permanently tuned to the soccer channel, and you probably wear soccer jerseys under your button-down shirt.' I've looked up hundreds of definitions online of the term 'passion,' and this one from Vocabulary.com struck me hard.

It was unbelievable, during the TLS, how everybody, especially the members of the group I was in, was so passionate. All of us volunteered to stay up late to finish the work given to us. And the students did not hesitate to have fun either. Every night, the clock would reach 3 a.m., and soft laughter would still be heard from the dorm rooms. We would all spread out in the common room on the first floor to have meetings on the big project we were working on for Ms. Lee's class, to finish up the speech for Mr. Tarnowski's workshop or to deal with Mr. Lim's negotiation work. Every single part of our bodies ached when we reached the final day, but it was clear that everybody went home satisfied.

I.O.I.P.—Promoting Trilateral Interaction

I.O.I.P. is a brand new organization that our team members came up with during the 'Design Thinking' workshop. We were instructed to solve a problem that the youth of China, Japan and Korea were experiencing. Our team saw the career issue that the youth are dealing with as an overlapping problem raised in all three countries. After sharing each country's stance on the matter, we reached an agreement that most adults with jobs find it hard to recommend their jobs, which means they are not happy with their careers. So we set a goal: Let's make a future in which everybody is happy with his or her job.

As a Korean, I know what Korean society is like. Almost all high school students have no idea what to do when they grow up, adults find their jobs unpleasing, and students are always told only to study rather than to experience the real world. Focusing on the last issue, we decided to give students opportunities to explore various careers through internships. I.O.I.P. will first develop a partnership with corporations and organizations in China, Japan and Korea, which will enable future internship exchange programs. Then I.O.I.P. will establish various programs that will help students choose which internship would be appropriate for their interests. For example, those who are interested in science and engineering could work as assistants in laboratories; those who want to study art and history could work in museums with curators, preparing to be museum tour guides; and so on. In addition, the program will provide English-speaking students with advantages by allowing them to apply to all three countries (the international program), whereas those who speak only their mother language will be assigned to their own countries (the domestic program).

Although we knew at once that the education system in each country needs to be modified, our lack of authority and power to reform the education systems made us seek a compromise. We decided that it would be best for us to develop an internship program for the students in order to provide them with a real-life experience in the professional world. I got the idea from a book about a French boy doing an internship—in France, completing internships as a student is common. But coming up with the idea was the easy part. Ms. Lee, Mr. Lim, Mr. Kim and other Teaching Fellows who listened to the I.O.I.P. proposal gave us helpful feedback.

During the process of establishing the idea and organizing a presentation explaining the I.O.I.P, our group made a Facebook page. Building it symbolized an oath that all the group members took: one day, when one of the members is financially and mentally mature, he or she will try out this fantastic idea for real.

We played hard, worked hard and bonded hard. It was a priceless opportunity, meeting such passionate people, and I cross my fingers that in the future I will meet others like them. Thank you for being the most awesome partners, Annie Lee, David Liu, Donghee Seo, Kento Nakamoto and Tatsuro Murakami.

Lesson 4: Perfect Teachers

Back in my school, it was rare to witness students, as well as teachers, speaking up first in class, let alone giving instant feedback to classmates. However, in the TLS, students were raising their hands in the air every time. Ms. Lee, a lovely instructor who challenged us all the time, asked questions that required deep and creative thinking. She made me think of more and more creative answers until eventually she was satisfied with the answers. I was used to giving short answers without any explanation, such as 'I prefer to read novels.' But Ms. Lee asked for more, so in the end my answers were abundant with facts, such as 'The first book I encountered was *Harry Potter*, which led me to a whole new universe. Since my first impression of those novels was great, I started reading more and more, for example *Percy Jackson*, *The Giver*, etc. For those reasons, I prefer to read novels rather than comic books. Comic books are not bad, but, personally, I find that the drawings lack capability in describing the exact situation of the story, as compared to writing.'

There was another teacher named Mr. Tarnowski. One special thing I still remember about him is that he always took notes while students were delivering speeches. Unlike Ms. Lee, he would wait until he got answers from the whole class before giving his feedback. While he was giving his feedback, he would point to each person, offering his thoughts on their ideas or sympathizing with the students' answers by explaining one of his own experiences. All of the accuracy in his answers came from his note taking habit and his powerful concentration on his students.

I know that role playing is the best method to acquire new skills. Mr. Kim proved that this is true with his workshop on 'Negotiation Leadership.' I was able to pair up with another student, and together we acted as if we were in an actual situation, negotiating a contract. Mr. Kim showed us how to greet our opponent, including great details like the handshake, how to appeal to the other person's sympathy, and how to read his or her face to make the deal more successful.

I had never considered negotiating as an everyday activity before, but through the lesson, it became clear that negotiation skills are necessary in achieving one's goals in life.

The teacher who inspired me most was Mr. Kralev. From him, I learned about 'Authentic Leadership.' During his lectures, students would freely raise their hands and tell their experiences with the topic, and if students were misdirected, Mr. Kralev would lead us to the right path with instant feedback. He is the Macedonian I mentioned above who often talked about his global life experiences. Thanks to him, I got back on track: before I had been frustrated about the matter of studying abroad. He suggested that I study in Europe rather than spending a fortune in other countries that have high tuition rates. From his words and tone, it wasn't hard to see his sincere concern for his students. He would say something like this: 'There's no need to be obsessed with grades. Life has more to offer than studying.'

I hope my reflection will show all the lessons I have learned: Respect those who are different from you. Be passionate about what you love. Never judge a person by their external skills. And lastly, there are many people whom you can look up to.

For all the wonderful experiences, I thank my dear teacher and also a friend, Kelsey, for providing me with the opportunity in the first place. The people I met during the TLS were the most passionate people I have ever encountered in my life, and I will remember them as the wonderful people who made me what I am today. The feedback I got from the teachers will be treasured forever. I solemnly wish that the TLS unit will remain one in the upcoming future.

| Chapter 21 |

From a Personal Point of View to a Global Vision

Hinako Telengut

● ● ●

I learned many things and gained a lot of great friends from the TLS, which was held in Korea for five days. Since I took part in this program and learned the skills that are needed to be a leader who will lead Asia in the future, I have been strongly conscious of three things that leaders must do.

Before attending the Summit, while I knew the benefits of the program, and though I was eager to participate in it, one memory made the decision to submit the registration form difficult. This one thing made me feel inferior when communicating with other people. Let me tell you about my memory and the reasons why it made the choice difficult.

Four years ago, when I started studying English in my junior high school, I took part in a program held by EC Cambridge because I wanted to improve my English. Of course, there were many other students who wanted to learn English as well. Many of them were from Europe, and the delegates were thirteen to seventeen years old. Though I wanted to make friends, I could not find any in the first week, and I could not identify the reasons for my failure. I thought of many possible explanations, imagining that maybe my personality was gloomy or that my story was not exciting, or even that my appearance was problematic. I thought and thought, but I could not reach the answer. And that made me really sad. Nevertheless, I never gave up trying to make friends. A week passed, and then one day I found a girl who seemed to be from Europe having lunch alone. I decided to approach her. Surprisingly and happily, we clicked and stayed friends. She was from Switzerland. My efforts bore fruit, finally! Both of us were really happy. She was the first, the only and the most important friend of mine at that time, and she is one of my best friends even now.

This memory made the choice to apply to the TLS difficult for me. I was scared of being hurt again. However, I then remembered 'the first, the only and the most important friend.' If you never give up and keep making an effort, you can overcome your difficulties and you will see success someday and somewhere. I was driven by that motivation, and I decided to submit my application to the TLS program. I had also never thought about the concept of 'leadership' as this is a really new idea in Japan. We can't even directly translate it into Japanese, so we use the character 'katakana' to express it. 'Katakana' is usually used for words that have come to Japan from abroad, and many of their exact meanings don't exist in Japanese. I told myself, 'You have to lead yourself and go challenge yourself before finishing high school!' That is why I decided to participate in TLS. It wasn't an irrelevant dream; I had a very personal reason.

I was very fortunate to be elected as one of the members of this program. The TLS was the most excellent program that I have ever participated in. Thanks to the Teaching Fellows and Student Leaders, I learned many new things and made many great friends in the program. Each of the delegates talked to me frankly throughout the five days. My worries disappeared as soon as the program started. The delegates were not only interested in establishing improved relations among our three countries—China, Korea and Japan—they also had interests in countries besides their own. We keep in touch even now. I was also able to recognize the existence of serious world problems, such as gender and racial discrimination, and poverty. These are words not usually heard in Japan, and I thus expanded my view of society, which was a precious as well as a shocking experience for me. Lastly, I gained countless beneficial skills and knowledge from the TLS lectures.

Before I wrote this essay, I used Ms. Lee's method of brainstorming and found it very useful. It remained in my memory from the time when we discussed what we needed for establishing better trilateral relationships during presentations on our last day. The brainstorming process that Ms. Lee taught us worked like this: write down all the things you come up with in a limited amount of time. In the high school I go to, teachers often make us brainstorm, but they do not tell us how to do it. Before I took Ms. Lee's class, I did not know the sense and purpose of doing it. Now I know that brainstorming is one of the most efficient ways to reach my own answers. In addition, I learned many things from my group. During our discussion, I learned to speak out and tell each member what I wanted to say. In our talks, each of us could understand deeply. For instance, I hadn't realized before that famous Japanese actors and actresses and even playwrights are also famous in China and Korea.

The negotiation method that Mr. Kim taught us was also very helpful, not only in financial exchanges but also in discussions in my school that do not involve money. The things that Mr. Kim taught were very practical: do not start by talking about money, reflect on the solution that will satisfy each of you and do not forget gratitude. I could apply these already. An English speech contest will be held in my school next January, and some debates will be held between two groups; each one will involve a discussion in front of all the other students and teachers. Each of my team members researched and brought both consenting and adverse opinions on our topic: 'Junk food should be banned from schools.' The other day, we had to pick out a few ideas as our strongest opinions. The negotiating time was easy because our 'Zone of Possible Agreement' (ZOPA) included those ideas that could compete effectively against the other team's opinion. However, each of us insisted that our own opinion was the most important. When it was my turn during that discussion, I asserted that my opinion was one of the most remarkable because I had found an American article that said, 'Eating junk food has the same effects as drug abuse.' Finally, my opinion was selected.

The lesson that I learned in '21st Century Skills and Attributes,' taught by Mr. Lim, was really interesting. Mr. Lim gave us many fascinating games to play in his class. Though it was difficult for me, the Oil Company game was the one I enjoyed the most. In that game, each of us was the owner of an oil company and could decide to make our oil prices Higher or Lower. There were four or five oil company owners in each group.

If this many countries price LOW:	If this many countries price HIGH:	Then countries pricing LOW:	And countries pricing HIGH:
4 price LOW	0 price HIGH	Lose 10 million each	
3 price LOW	1 prices HIGH	Win 10 million each	Lose 30 million
2 price LOW	2 price HIGH	Win 20 million each	Lose 20 million each
1 prices LOW	3 price HIGH	Win 30 million	Lose 10 million each
0 price LOW	4 price HIGH		Win 10 million each

As you see, you will surely win if you keep choosing a Lower price. However, if your group members believe each other and no one break the promise always to price High, nobody loses and everyone wins. Needless to say, however, though that is the ideal way, it doesn't often come off. Someone will usually tell a lie. During that game, I came to understand why we do not do well in my class at school: no one acts as a leader and each of us says what we want to say without thinking about the overall situation. I learned that you should grasp your teammates' ways of thinking and their personalities. When I get a chance to participate in another project like the TLS, I want to gain trust and be one of the essential members without forgetting to 'go to the balcony,' or, in other words, take a step back to evaluate the larger situation.

Mr. Tarnowski taught me communication skills, which are very important for my future, since to be involved in the science world has been my longing since childhood. To have good presentations skill is essential for scientists not only to gain research funds by conveying the importance of their studies but also to present their research results. In Mr. Tarnowski's class, we watched good examples and bad ones. We also learned that those people who have good speech skills will do well in achieving their aims. All of the delegates presented splendid four-minute speeches. I tried hard to do my best in my four-minute speech. I am eager to use these skills again—giving concrete examples with passion that can be remembered by my audience, and offering logical and realistic opinions—in my school's English Speech Contest next year.

I learned several skills that leaders need from the TLS. First, to come up with innovative and beneficial ideas that can create solutions to a problem, and to exploit your team's abilities to make the project a success. Second, to grasp your environment and understand the teammates that you have to get along with. Third, to be trusted by your teammates. And lastly, to present your thoughts well so that your audience can understand your opinions exactly.

Each class had a connection with the other classes. Communication skills, which Mr. Tarnowski taught us, are used widely as a tool for negotiation, which we learned about from Mr. Kim. Preparing for our presentations with Ms. Lee helped us to go 'onto the balcony' with Mr. Lim. Negotiation can be utilized for not only in the TLS but outside. In addition, I have become strongly conscious of three things that Asian leaders should do, the reasons why they should do them and how we can deal with them.

First, I realized how important understanding is during Ms. Lee's class. Many Asians have only a slight or superficial understanding of other Asian countries, but that is not enough for mutual understanding. Therefore, leaders should encourage mutual understanding to strengthen the unity of Asia. There should be an increase in the number of programs that help people learn about their cultures, the daily lives of their citizens and the living and social environments. People should be encouraged to visit not only the urban areas that are developed but also the countryside in each nation. The government of each country could provide support; for example, the Japanese Official Development Assistance provides funding and technological assistance to peace building, governance, propulsion of fundamental human rights and 'development' involving humanitarian aid for developing countries and international organizations. If we could achieve these three aims and grasp their strong and weak points from a neutral, comprehensive, and detailed standpoint, it will become much easier to build cooperative relations among the different countries.

Second, I think that the assistance to Asia's development today from major developed countries, such as the U.K., France, Germany, Sweden, the U.S., Canada and Australia does not reach real, extreme poverty. In Mr. Tarnowski's class, one boy, who is from Malaysia, told us about a girl he knows who is a prostitute in need. I was really moved by his story. In order for outside aid to solve fundamental problems in Asia, individuals who live in Europe or America must understand Asian realities. This will be especially helpful because individuals sometimes initiate actions faster than governments, helping those who are in trouble more efficiently. Programs such as the one described above would allow for people who live outside Asia to participate in or establish organizations or systems that allow Asian citizens to obtain financial or material assistance. When we can achieve these goals, I think that the assistance from outside Asia for developing Asia will expand.

Third, I learned from the TLS that there aren't enough human resources available today to develop Asia. It is essential to educate people who can be the next generation of leaders in order to achieve our aims. In my opinion, productive programs like this one should be held in as many countries as possible to give opportunities to everyone to be leaders, regardless of their nationalities or residential preferences. Establishing educational institutions will expand and foster human resources efficiently.

Though my opinions as described above are elementary, I know that developing a conscious 'leadership' mentality is just as important as actually leading people. And now, after the TLS, I can look at the world with a wider view. I have reflected on my experience in the U.K. In hindsight, I was fortunate to have had a lonely time and difficult experiences communicating because positive results sometimes stem from negative situations. The TLS allowed me to think about things in a more realistic and wide-ranging way, just like a reflecting mirror. If you have a negative experience, it can lead to a positive view. I appreciate the TLS, which allowed me to take a step back and look at our world, Asia, my own country and even myself. In the future, if I have a chance to face an international problem and to negotiate it, I will first remember my TLS experience, my friends from more than three countries, the Teaching Fellows, the Student Leaders and their intellectual passion.

This Summit also led me to think about international relationships. If I ever take on a leadership role in an organization, I will try to think in the way that the TLS taught me when I face my troubles.

I will try to use different methods to speculate and thus find solutions to various issues, and to remember that the most important things are how I lead myself and how I organize my thinking and search for knowledge. I am very grateful that I have departed from a personal point of view and that the TLS guided me to find a new vision from the perspective of globalization. When the Teaching Fellows led us in the lectures and discussions, we suddenly found ourselves looking at the globalized view, and we became the leaders of our communities almost without noticing. Also, we were able to take a step back to reflect about our own countries, the world and our own futures.

Finally, I want to mention three things that I will need to be one of the next leaders. First, I will talk a lot with the good friends and teachers I met in this program in order to grow. Second, I will keep in mind, the existence of people who are in real poverty. Third, I will never give up working hard to be a real leader. I really appreciate all of the great friends, great Teaching Fellows and great Student Leaders I have met. I was very happy to participate in this program. My choice led me to my fortune. I think that our choices are important: the choice I made when I decided to take part in the TLS made me grow as a human being. In the *Harry Potter* movies, Headmaster Dumbledore says at one point to Harry: 'It is our choices that show what we truly are, far more than our abilities.' We have to make a lot of choices every day. I want to remember that we have to use our abilities and wisdom to make the right choice.

I will never forget this irreplaceable 2016 summer. I would like to thank my Teaching Fellows, Student Leaders and a lot of good friends. I was very lucky to be able to participate in the TLS which was one of the most meaningful programs I have ever participated.

Many valuable lessons that the Teaching Fellows taught me have brought me new confidence. Thank you all for everything.

| Editor's Acknowledgments |

●●●

As the editor of this book, and on behalf of the Asia Leadership Institute, I would like to extend our gratitude to the many people who made the Asia Leadership Youth (ALY) Camp in Malaysia, Global Leadership Trek (GLT) in the U.S., Central Asia Youth Leadership Camp (CALC) co-organized by the Korea Development Bank (KDB) Foundation in Pohang, Korea, and Trilateral Leadership Summit III (TLS) in Incheon, Korea a reality.

To all the participants, with whom I spent an unforgettable time teaching, mentoring, and in the process becoming lifelong partners for the greater cause of the public – Janice Tan Sue Wei, Michelle S Lee, Bryan Chay, Jonson Tham, Ben Ang Zi Qi, Kamaleshwaran Ganeson, Ong Qian Chern, Loh Lynn Way, Mengheng Lim, Maika Tsuchiya, Amirhossein Rahbari, Aleksandra Kan, Anastasiia Lun, Anjela Kamalova, Evgeniy Kim, Zarina Shemdanova, Megumi Konishi, Annie Dawon Lee, Shiina Yuri, Jiho Hwang, Alex Wookyung Lee, and Hinako Telengut.

To the Teaching Fellows who graciously offered their instruction, advice, and mentorship at the programs – Ms. Lisa Lee, Ed.M., Harvard Graduate School of Education (HGSE); Mr. Randy Tarnowski,

Ed.M, HGSE; Mr. John Lim, MALD, Fletcher School of Law and Diplomacy; Mr. John Lee, MCMPA, Harvard Kennedy School of Government (HKSG); and Mr. Panche Kralev, MCMPA, HKSG. They have been such a caring, thoughtful and inspiring group of people to work with. I am truly humbled by their dedication and service, and the depth of their knowledge.

To members of the Organizing Committee of the ALY Camp: Ms. Carol Wong, Mr. Dencoln Tan, Ms. Nikki Ong, Ms. Shannon D. Francis, Ms. Gan Shan Xin, and Mr. Tan Zhi Kai. To the Student Leaders of the ALY Camp: Ryan Lee Juin Jie, Ellen Chai Voon Kah, Lee Wai Leong, Tan Dun Yuan, Yeoh Guan Aik, Tan Wei Shan, Bong Gin Teen, Seow Ijay, Marian Yeow Chee Yen, and Low Kai Jie.

To those from the Sunway Group, Dr. Jeffrey Cheah, Founder and Chairman of Sunway Group; Dr. See-Yan Lin, President of the Harvard Club of Malaysia; Dr. Weng Keng Lee, CEO of Education and Healthcare Division; Dr. Elizabeth Lee, Senior Executive Director of the Sunway Education Group; Ms. Mien Wee Cheng, Executive Director of the Sunway International School; and Ms. Beng Lean Ng, Director of the Office of the Senior Executive Director, as well as other teachers and administrative staff who took part in making the ALY Camp a success.

I would also like to extend my sincere gratitude to those who have given us support in many ways from sparing their precious time to meet with us, to offering us venues and residences for the programs. For the GLT, I would like to thank Mr. Ryan Allen and Ms. April Bang, Ph.D Candidates at the Columbia University Teacher's College; Ms. Ruth Shillingford, Acting Justice at the New York Supreme Court; Ms. Anika Price, Court Attorney at the NYS Office of Court

Administration; Ms. Sharon Bourne Clarke at the New York City Civil Court; Ms. Elizabeth Kallop, Strategy Specialist, Ms. Danielle Huddleston and Ms. Mai Lynn Miller Nguyen, both program directors at the Open Society Foundations; Ms. Kristine Lin, Program Director at the Fulbright Foundation; Mr. Scott Beale, CEO, Mr. Andrew Tangas, Ms. Linda Keene Solomon, and Ms. Kelly Reid from the Atlas Corps; Ms. Clare Carlo, Research Associate at Hager Associates; Mr. Jae Yun from the Capital Guidance, Ms. Charlene Hasib from the Federal Reserve Bank of the U.S., Ms. Shalini Sharan from Willis Towers Watson, Ms. Sookyung Koo, Executive Director at the International Leadership Foundation; Mr. Barry M. Hager, Attorney and President of Hager Associates; Ms. Nancy Yuan, Vice President of the Asia Foundation; Dr. Gil Alterovitz, Assistant Professor at the Harvard Medical School; Ms. Becky Moore from the Philips Exeter Academy; and Ms. Erin Lynn, Director of the Integrated Heritage Project. Institutions wise, the admission offices of the Georgetown University, George Washington University, Harvard University, Massachusetts Institute of Technology, Princeton University, Yale University, and Columbia University.

For the CALC, I would like to thank Ms. Jung Jiyu, Program Director at the KDB Foundation; Mr. Daniel Kim and Mr. Seonhan Kim, Directors of the Handong Global Academy; our Russian translators, Mr. Vladimir Samsonov and Mr. Eugene Kramov; and the eight Student Leaders and supporting staff.

For the TLS, the senior leadership team of Youth Union of Politics and Diplomacy (YUPAD); Mr. Jiro Yoshino, Country Director of Japan for CALI; Mr. Ozawa Akihiro, Director of Route H, Benesse Corporation; Mr. Russell Saito, Program Head of the Impact Japan

Foundation; Katie Yao, Director of the St. Bell Education Group; Dr. Emanuel Pastreich, Associate Professor at Kyung Hee University and Director of the Asia Institute; and leadership teams at the State University of New York Korea and George Mason University Korea, including Mr. Taewan Kim, Executive Director of Marketing and Student Recruitment at Ghent, without whom we would not have pulled this program together.

Working on this book requires a huge amount of time and effort especially in the early stages of the process. A special thanks to Ms. Ida Fazila Ismail, Head of Acumen Case Center at CALI Malaysia for overseeing the writing and content for this book, and enforcing quality editorial standards when necessary.

Last but not least, my wonderful team at CALI Boston, Ms. Ursula DeYoung, Advisor of Publication Affairs, and CALI Malaysia: Dr. Gin Chee Tong, Head of Strategy and Management; Ms. Jocelyn Lew En Mei, Strategy and Management Executive, Ms. Farzeera Emir, Executive Assistant to President; and the Center's interns, Michelle S Lee and Serena Kaan, deserve immense credit for the many hours spent putting this book together for print.

Thank you all for your hard work, support and leadership.

Program Details

● ● ●

I. Asia Leadership Youth (ALY) Camp

High school students are at a juncture in which their decisions, attitudes, and habits play a crucial role in shaping the rest of their lives. Those growing up in Malaysia face particular challenges as their society evolves and foundational values face a more modern, global context. Leadership begins with self-awareness of one's personality, character, and values. It then translates into personal growth and one's ability to work with others to tackle common challenges whether it be in family, school, or community.

"Developing a Powerful Personal Brand" and "Developing a Successful Career Path" are the themes for the Asia Leadership Institute's Asia Leadership Youth and Scholars 2016 programs. It features workshops in leadership, public speaking, and practical skills, seminars on professional development and applying to overseas universities, as well as special talks and networking opportunities. The program aims to help young people prepare for the leadership challenges they will face in their personal, professional, and communal life, as well as help them translate their values into action, and that action into meaningful and material value for others.

Values into Action: A Practical Program for Emerging Leaders of Social Change

A. Participants Engage in Workshops on (a) Leadership and Communications, (b) Innovation and Problem Solving. Participants will have the opportunity to attend two (2) four-session workshops on the themes of:

Leadership and Communications

The first set of workshops focuses on increasing participants' capacity to lead through adaptive pressure, as well as to communicate effectively in diverse settings. Participants will practice the skills and mindsets associated with the framework of adaptive leadership, leadership communications, and overcoming immunity to change. The methods of instruction include a mixture of the case method of instruction, case-in-point teaching, and structured exercises.

Innovation and Practical Skills

The second set of workshops focuses on the capacity to approach problems with a set of frameworks and tools to solve through innovative thinking. Instructors will introduce the frameworks and concepts of design thinking, rapid prototyping, value creation, and trust building in collaborative environments. The methods of instruction include a mixture of the case method of instruction, structured exercises and experiential simulations.

B. Special "TED" Talks that Highlight Themes of Leadership, Innovative Practices, and Global Trends. Our fellows come from diverse walks of life and expertise and are eager to share their knowledge and experience in the form of special, short talks.

C. CALI Talk Show Forum. Modelled after the JFK Jr. Forum at the Harvard Kennedy School, the Forum is organized as a talk show and panel discussion in which Fellows or local experts and personalities sit on a panel and are interviewed on a focusing topic relevant to our audience, local participants may be chosen to act as a moderator of the forum.

D. Culminating Pitch Competition. The competition is an experiential exercise in which students prepare during the camp and compete on the last day of the program. Through the competition, they will apply persuasion principles to a particular personal and professional interest or idea. They will have the opportunity to persuade other participants and instructors about a professional topic that they are passionate about and hope to accomplish.

E. Networking. Networking opportunities with CALI Fellows and distinguished leaders in the fields of business, government, and society.

F. Asia Leadership Youth (ALY) Camp Schedule

	MON	TUE	WED	THU	FRI	SAT
8:00am	Registration & Breakfast	Preparation and Breakfast				Community Service Ceremony & Breakfast
9:00am	Welcoming Ceremony & Orientation	Speech Competition				
10:00am	Break					
10:10am	Plenary Session: Personal Branding and Career Building					
11:30am	Break					Community Service Day and Commitment Letter & Debrief
11:40am	Plenary Session: Entrepreneurial Leadership A					
12:40pm	Lunch Break					
1:20pm	Plenary Session: Entrepreneurial Leadership B					
2:40pm	Break					
2:50pm	Workshop Session A: Leadership					
3:50pm	Break					
4:00pm	Workshop Session B: Innovation					Check-out
5:00pm	Break					

	MON	TUES	WED	THU	FRI	SAT
5:10pm	Career Mentoring	Professional Development	Special Talk	Professional Development	Sunway Lagoon Wildlife Encounter	Graduation Dinner
6:00pm	Break					
6:15pm	Sunway Pyramid Ice	Captain Ball	Dialogue in the Dark	Zumba		
7:15pm	Dinner & Free Time					
8:30pm	Homework					

II. Global Leadership Trek (GLT)

The two-week Global Leadership Trek (GLT) is inspired by the Asia Leadership Trek (ALT), the Center for Asia Leadership Initiatives' (CALI) flagship program since 2012. Like the Asia Leadership Trek for scholars at Harvard, the GLT is a unique, overseas firsthand learning experience comprised of a socioeconomic, political and cultural study and leadership training tour to the three cities in the United States. As a program catered exclusively to the needs of young emerging leaders in Asia, the Global Leadership Trek culminates in a leadership camp, designed specifically to help participants understand the U.S. university application process, and gain new understanding and skills to practice effective leadership for the 21st century.

For GLT 2016, the students traveled to New York, Washington D.C. and Boston. In its first stop, they experienced some of New York's finest – from contemporary marvels like the Statue of Liberty and the Empire State Building, to the United Nations Headquarters, a pinnacle of modern democracy. They also made stops at Columbia University and Princeton University; both ranked among the top five universities in the United States. Next, they went to Washington D.C., the capital of the United States, to make memorable visits to the White House, Capitol Hill, Lincoln Memorial, among others. Also included was a visit to Georgetown University, the oldest Catholic and Jesuit institution of higher education in the United States. The last destination – Boston – is globally revered as the international center of higher education. The highlights included a visit to Harvard University, as well as to other renowned institutions like MIT, Babson College and The Phillips School. In Boston, they experienced a transformational leadership camp.

Global Leadership Trek (GLT) Schedule

AUG	ACTIVITIES			
15	Rockefeller Center Tour	Central Park	Statue of Liberty Tour	Empire State Building
16	Columbia University Tour	Cloister Museum	National Museum of History	
17	Princeton University Tour	Dialogue with Ryan Allen, Ph.D. Candidate and Researcher at Columbia University Teacher's College		

18	Visit and Panel Discussion at Open Society Foundations	United Nations Tour	Meeting with Admissions Officers	Dialogue and Dinner with April Bang, Instructor of Leadership, Ph.D. Candidate at Columbia University Teacher's College
19	Travel to DC	Atlas Corps		
20	Georgetown University Tour	Air & Space Museum		
21	Arlington Cemetery	Newseum	Study Time	
22	International Leadership Foundation	Meetings with Professors and Admissions Officers at Georgetown University		
23	White House	Washington Monument	Capitol Hill Special Tour	Networking Event with Young Professionals
24	Depart to Boston	Harvard University Kennedy School Tour	Harvard Medical School Tour	Dialogue and Dinner with Prof. Gil Alterovitz
25	MIT Tour	Boston Duck Tour		
26	Philips Exeter Academy Tour	Harvard Business School Tour		
27	Leadership Program by John Lim, John Lee, and Hungsoo S. Kim			
28	Boston Red Sox Baseball Game			
29	Yale University Tour	Depart to NYC	Depart Home	

III. Central Asia Youth Leadership Camp (CALC)

The Central Asia Youth Leadership Camp (CALC) is a collaboration between the Center for Asia Leadership Initiatives (CALI) and the Korea Development Bank Foundation to benefit young leaders in Central Asia.

A. Speech Competition

Effectively communicating as a leader means engaging those around you through the use of stories that binds and motivates people through common cause. It is first a "story of self": communicating who I am: my values, my experience, why I do what I do. Secondly, it is a "story of us" communicating who we are: our shared values, our shared experience, and why we do what we do. And lastly, it is a "story of now" articulating the present as a moment of challenge, choice, and hope. Based on research and courses conducted at the Harvard Kennedy School on the leadership frameworks and communication techniques of the most effective leaders – this workshop trains participants on essential leadership principles, while allowing them to practice proven communication techniques.

Randy Tarnowski

B. Special Talk

How is your mindset affecting your ability to lead?
Is your mindset affecting your ability to lead? At this talk, Randy

Tarnowski discusses recent research which he and other Harvard University researchers have conducted on the relationship between social networks and growth mindset. He presents four important advantages for leaders in business, education and politics by instilling a growth mindset in your team.

Randy Tarnowski

C. Plenary Sessions

1. Developing a Powerful Personal Brand and Building a Successful Career Path

Executive positive change is never an easy task. Many youths have the desire to stand out and excel, but may be unsure what they could do to leave a positive mark on the world. For youths on the threshold of adulthood, ever present for 21st century citizens are concerns about one's readiness to take on personal and professional responsibilities, and how to become a talent of great value and develop a successful career path.

Using leadership frameworks taught at Harvard University, participants will be challenged to dig deep and discover their hidden strengths and address shortcomings, how to create opportunities to make meaningful progress with their strengths and passions, and achieve a healthier self-worth by turning downsides into upsides, They will also have the opportunity to identify their core values, strengths, passion and 'true colors', build and mold the right mindset and skillsets to make meaningful progress by turning downsides into upsides, and develop a strategic plan to build a successful path.

Hungsoo S. Kim

2. Entrepreneurial Leadership

What does it take to be an effective leader in today's fast paced and ever-changing society? Unfortunately, the answer does not lie in principles or frameworks, or five easy steps to be a great leader. To become an effective leader for the future, one needs to hone in and refine specific skill sets to quickly adapt to a changing environment and take advantage of the opportunities it offers. Skills like Critical Thinking, Collaboration, Communication, Creative Problem solving are considered key 21st century skills that cultivate the kind of mindset that is needed to succeed. This workshop is structured to engage, equip, and apply these skills using real case-studies, discussions, and exercises.

Session A will utilize the case method, practiced widely at Harvard, to analyze real life scenarios of entrepreneurial leaders and the skills they effectively applied to achieve their goals.

Session B will apply design thinking principles as well as lessons from cases to brainstorm, ideate, design, and prototype an innovative solution to a problem of each group's choosing.

From these sessions, students will learn and apply strategies for effective teamwork, problem solving skills, principles for casting a powerful vision, elements of persuasive communication, and entrepreneurial leadership.

Lisa Lee

D. Professional Development

These study group sessions are designed to advance participants' ancillary capabilities in verbal, written, and professional areas by providing them with knowledge, best practices, and skillsets that will help them in their personal, academic, and professional life. These sessions are drawn from Teaching Fellows' expertise and experience in applying to U.S. universities and applying for careers in a Western and International context.

Applying to US Universities:
Hungsoo S. Kim/ Randy Tarnowski
Finding and Choosing the Program
Right for You
Admissions Essay: The Statement of
Purpose

Communication Skills:
John Lim/ Lisa Lee
Interviewing Skills
Writing Skills

E. Career Mentoring

Facilitators take the role of a career counselor and share their experiences with the purpose of helping students gain insight into their own possible career paths. Facilitators will represent these areas:

John Lim
Research, Policy, & Foreign Service

Lisa Lee
Finance

Panche Kralev

Telecommunications & Government

Randy Tarnowski

Education & Non-Profit

Hungsoo S. Kim

Management Consulting

F. Workshop A: Leadership

1. Personal Leadership: Achieving Your Goal

In a world full of vision, strategy and goals that are regularly being cast for organizations, businesses, governments and the world, we too need a personal vision and plan of action for our own lives in order to find purpose, fulfilment and personal success. This workshop is focused on defining and clarifying your own personal purpose and translating that into actionable strategy for your current life stage. Participants will learn how to assess opportunities, evaluate options, hedge oneself against risk, and develop an action plan that works for them. By learning the tools to identify what one wants to accomplish and evaluate multiple courses of that can lead to purpose fulfillment-you will walk away with the self-confidence needed to succeed.

Lisa Lee

2. Authentic Leadership

Progress in our lives and careers will almost certainly involve situations which require us to take the lead. Not every decision taken at a point in time will provide the short term effects that we hope it has. Maintaining a long term perspective in these moments is crucial and we need a framework of understanding of the decision making process in order to effectively manage any situation. Cases of world leaders and entrepreneurs who have taken the lead in a variety of situations will set the context for understanding of the concept of leadership in challenging times.

Panche Kralev

3. Negotiation Leadership

Negotiation is often thought of as being in the realm of political and diplomatic leaders. But negotiation is a skill for one's everyday life. This workshop introduces the fundamentals of negotiation analysis and practice and will help participants develop a set of mindsets that will help them better analyze and prepare more effectively for any negotiation. Through participation in simulations, participants will have the opportunity to practice their powers of communication and persuasion, and to experiment with a variety of negotiation tactics and strategies. The aim of the workshop is to provide participants with a set of concepts and tools that they can apply immediately, in effect, helping them to approach situations in personal and professional life more intentionally and intelligently.

Hungsoo S. Kim

G. Workshop B: Innovation

1. 21st Century Skills and Attributes

The 21st century has brought a new kind of workplace, in which individuals are encountered with complex multidisciplinary, open-ended problems that don't come in multiple-choice formats or ready-made, standard solutions. Through lectures, strategic games, simulations, and case discussions, this workshop will enable participants to learn the mindsets and practice the skills needed to walk into settings and tackle complex problems. Individuals will find ways to uncover the purpose and possibility hidden in problems; they will then learn steps to diagnose the group dynamics they are operating in; they will then devise ways to strategically approach others with a mindset towards creating value rather than claiming value: lastly, they will deploy themselves through purposeful communications that mobilizes action.

John Lim

2. Introduction to Entrepreneurship

When we think of entrepreneurship, we think of starting a business. But entrepreneurship begins as a way of thinking strategically about any challenge. This has been the starting point on how the most successful entrepreneurs have developed the most innovative solutions to the world's most pressing problems. In this workshop, students will engage in case study discussions and lectures to build contextualized and experiential knowledge in aspects of entrepreneurship: mission and vision, positioning. funding and resources as well as impact and measurement. Crucially, participants will develop relevant skillsets in these areas through hands-on activities and simulations. At the end of this workshop, participants will be better equipped to approach and lead a new entrepreneurial venture as an independent start-up or within a large organization.

Panche Kralev

3. Cross-Cultural Competencies

Navigating groups and teams across cultural boundaries is critical for success in virtually any field, particularly in our increasingly globalized world. Whether the challenge arises from differences along ethnic, organizational, or national lines – individuals are needed to employ successful strategies to bridge differences and help diverse groups make progress on collective challenges. In the context of this workshop, we will view cross cultural leadership as a process. Participants will acquire a deeper understanding of culture as norms, become more adept at approaching and diagnosing challenges that arise from differences in culture and values, as well as practice cross-cultural competencies through social learning exercises.

Randy Tarnowski

H. Central Asia Youth Leadership Camp (CALC) Schedule

	SUN	MON	TUE	WED	THU
8:00am		Breakfast			
9:00am		Design Thinking Lectures			Small Group Entrepreneurship Exercise
10:20am		Break			
10:30am		Design Thinking Exercises			Small Group Activity
11:30am		Break			
11:40am		Workshop Session A			Entrepreneurship Presentations
1:00pm		Lunch			
2:00pm	Opening and Orientation (2:30pm)	Workshop Session B			Career Mentoring
3:20pm		Break			
3:30pm	Design Thinking Introduction	Design Exercise	Special Lecture / Workshop Session B	Special Forum Q&A	Final Presentation
4:50pm		Break			
5:10pm	Design Thinking Activity	Small Group Activity			Closing Ceremony
6:30pm		Dinner			

IV. Trilateral Leadership Summit III (TLS)

The TLS is an international program designed for Chinese, Japanese, and Korean high school youth to meaningfully tackle an emerging leadership challenge the Northeast Asia region is facing.

It is modelled after the U.S. Congress and Law Making and adaptive leadership courses at the Harvard Kennedy School of Government; it uses Stanford's design thinking approach, and is influenced by the Model UN Simulation.

A. Historical Overview
Trilateral Leadership Summit I
- November 12-15, 2014
- UNESCO Peace Center, Icheon, Korea
- In collaboration with: YUPAD
- Supported by: Asia Foundation, Northeast Asia History Foundation

Trilateral Leadership Summit II
- August 18-23, 2015
- Sendai Ikuei Gakeun High School, Sendai, Japan
- In collaboration with: Intilaq, St. Bell Investments
- Supported by: Harvard University Asia Center, U.S. Embassy Tomodachi Initiative, Route H-Benesse, Rotary Club, Korean Embassy in Japan, Prudential Insurance

B. Content Overview

The future of one's country and region lie in the hands of its young people. The opportunities for global leadership, and the potential to be the most prosperous region in the world, are ripe in Northeast Asia. But the region also faces challenges due to the geopolitical and strategic uncertainties surrounding its complex historical and territorial issues.

This four-night, five-day program provides young representatives from Northeast Asia with the skillsets to lead in the 21st century. Using leadership frameworks taught at Harvard University, participants will gain a better understanding of the complexities and varying perspectives on inter-Northeast Asia relations, increase their leadership capacity and skill level through participations in discussions, simulations, and skill-building workshops, as well as develop a growth mind-set, inter-region friendships, and a global orientation.

Participants will engage in interactive workshops, professional development sessions and career mentoring with teaching faculty from Harvard University and Stanford University. The program also provides participants with the opportunity to undergo a trilateral summit simulation for inter-country dialogue, networking, awareness raising, and collaborative skill development.

By the end of the program, participants will gain practical knowledge, skills, and experience on leadership, public speaking, and problem solving, and be guided on how to develop the right mindset to pursue peace, common prosperity and leadership initiatives in their future respective fields, their home region, and around the world.

C. Who Should Attend

This program is ideal for high school, college and university students who aspire to:

- Learn about diplomacy and international relations;
- Increase their leadership capacity and skills in public speaking, conflict resolution, negotiation, and consensus-building;
- Engage in an interactive learning experience that promotes problem solving and design thinking.

D. Key Benefits

Through the program, participants will:

- Explore interdisciplinary frameworks for analyzing the current intra-regional challenges from on-the-balcony and dance-floor perspectives, and identify collaborative accelerators and inhibitors
- Build analytical and behavioral skills, and develop tools to foster and sustain an entrepreneurial approach and cross cultural approach to the problem
- Learn fundamental concepts and gain fresh insights on problem solving strategy
- Understand the difference in culture and crisis management practices from three-nation perspectives
- Develop a strong network of high achieving peers from different countries, interests and schools

E. The Program

Trilateral Leadership Summit Program
Simulation and Design Thinking Exercise based on Harvard Kennedy School Courses, the Stanford Design Thinking Method, as well as the Model UN simulation

Forum Talk or Talk Show	TED-style Talk	Workshops	Networking Event	Mentoring Session
Kennedy School-style Talk show that shares ideas, lessons, and takeaways	Sharing of personal stories that draws life lessons and wisdom to life	Modeled after courses at the Harvard Kennedy School, Business School, Law School, School of Education	Free-flowing session for acquaintance and mingling between audience groups, organizers, and moderators	Down-to-earth stories and advice on career-related experiences and topics

1. Workshops:
Cross-Cultural Competencies

Navigating groups and teams across cultural boundaries is critical for success in virtually any field, particularly in our increasingly globalized world. Whether the challenge arises from differences along ethnic, organizational, or national lines – individuals are needed to employ successful strategies to bridge differences and help diverse groups make progress on collective challenges. In the context of this workshop, we will view cross cultural leadership as a process. Participants will acquire a deeper understanding of culture as norms, become more adept at approaching and diagnosing challenges that arise from differences in culture and values, as well as practice cross-cultural competencies through social learning exercises.

Leadership Communications: Mobilizing for Change

Effectively communicating as a leader means engaging those around you through the use of stories that binds and motivates people through common cause. It is first a "story of self:" communicating who I am: my values, my experience, why I do what I do. Secondly, it is a "story of us" communicating who we are: our shared values, our shared experience, and why we do what we do. And lastly, it is a "story of now" articulating the present as a moment of challenge, choice, and hope. Based on research and courses conducted at the Harvard Kennedy School on the leadership frameworks and communication techniques of the most effective leaders – this workshop trains participants in essential leadership principles, while allowing them to practice proven communication techniques.

Introduction to Entrepreneurship

When we think of entrepreneurship, we think of starting a business. But entrepreneurship begins as a way of thinking strategically about any challenge. This has been the starting point on how the most successful entrepreneurs have developed the most innovative solutions to the world's most pressing problems. In this workshop, students will engage in case study discussions and lectures to build contextualized and experiential knowledge in aspects of entrepreneurship: mission and vision, positioning, funding and resources, as well as impact and measurement. Crucially, participants will develop relevant skillsets in these areas through hands-on activities and simulations. At the end of this workshop, participants will be better equipped to approach and lead a new entrepreneurial venture as an independent start-up or within a large organization.

2. Special Talks:
- Finding and Setting Priorities
- How Not to Lose Your Identity
- Finding Your Definition of Success
- Balancing Expectations While Pursuing Your Dreams
- Led or moderated by the Teaching Fellows, these sessions serve as an arena for discussion and debate on emerging topics of leadership, innovation, politics and education

3. Career Mentoring:
- Management Consulting
- Finance and Banking
- Entrepreneurship
- International Organizations
- These sessions see Teaching Fellows take the role of career counsellors to guide participants on their current or future career paths through the sharing of personal and professional experiences

4. Professional Development:
- Applying to US Universities
- Essential Presentation Skills
- Developing Your Personal Identity
- Transitioning from School to Work
- These topics are designed to advance participants' capacities in verbal, written and professional areas. Providing best practices that will help them in their personal, academic and professional life

F. Trilateral Leadership Summit III (TLS) Schedule

	SUN	MON	TUE	WED	THU
8:00am		Breakfast			
9:00am		The Practice of Negotiation			TLS Simulation Design Thinking Exercise
10:20am		Break			
10:30am		TLS Design Thinking Simulation A			Simulation Final Presentation
11:30am		Break			Clean and Pack-up
11:40am		TLS Design Thinking Simulation B			Lunch (12:15pm) and Bus Drop-off at Airport and Seoul (1:20pm)
1:00pm	Bus Pick-up at Airport and Arrival at IGC Venue	Lunch			
2:00pm		Workshop Session B			
3:20pm		Break			
3:30pm		Challenges and Opportunities in the 21st Century Northeast Asia	Workshop Session B		
4:50pm		Break			
5:10pm		Team Building Exercises			
6:30pm		Dinner			
7:30pm	Welcome Program	Workshop Session B	Incheon Global Campus Presentation	Professional Development Session & Career Mentoring	
8:30pm		Personal Time			

| Appendix II |

About the Teaching Faculty

● ● ●

Hungsoo S. Kim, *MPA, Harvard Kennedy School*

Hungsoo is the Co-founder and President of the Center for Asia Leadership Initiatives. Passionate about nurturing and empowering talents in Asia, he has developed and organized over twenty-five programs in more than twenty-two countries in the region to help budding leaders enhance their leadership competencies to navigate challenges in the 21st century. Hungsoo aims to engage with youth in all forty-eight countries in Asia by 2022 and inspire them to enact change in the world.

John Lim, *Tufts Fletcher School; Harvard Extension School*

John Lim is Co-founder and Managing Director of CALI Boston. A former fellow of the Harvard University Asia Center, he has worked in diverse organizations including the Embassy of Canada in Korea, the International Crisis Group, and in different sectors such as English education and social entrepreneurship. His current work engages him in researching and applying various leadership, education, and entrepreneurial models and frameworks within the Asian contexts.

John Lee, *MCMPA, Harvard Kennedy School*

John Lee came to the U.S. when he was a year old with his father, who was a Korean Diplomat. Mr. Lee grew up in New York City and graduated from Cornell University with a B.S. in Policy Analysis and Management. Following Cornell, Mr. Lee moved to Korea to become better versed in its history, language, and culture. He spent over a decade in Asia, working primarily with international NGOs, economic think tanks, and government ministries before completing a Masters in Public Administration at Harvard University's JFK School of Government. Prior to HKS, Mr. Lee worked for the U.S. State Department in the U.S. Embassy Seoul, leading programs on innovation and tech-focused research.

Panche Kralev, *MCMPA, Harvard Kennedy School*

Panche Kralev is currently serving as President of the Board of Directors of Macedonian Telekom (Deutsche Telekom Group). He is a former Minister of Education and Science and Advisor to the Prime Minister of the Republic of Macedonia. During his career he has also worked in investment banking part of Raiffeisen Investment and the SEAF equity fund. Mr. Kralev is a former Mason Fellow of the MPA at the Harvard Kenned School and brings insight into public policy, leadership and strategy.

Lisa Lee, *Ed.M., Harvard Graduate School of Education*

Lisa Lee is a recent graduate of Harvard Graduate School of Education, where she received her Master's degree in International Education Policy. She came to Harvard after teaching and consulting in Kazakhstan for nearly three years, where she started an initiative for university students to engage in critical issues in their immediate contexts. Previous to teaching, Ms. Lee worked on Wall Street as a global investment analyst and equity trader. Ms. Lee is a firm believer in taking all the and experiences at one's disposal and channeling them to make maximum impact. Her studies at Harvard focused on education and innovation, as well as entrepreneurial management. She founded the Harvard Graduate School of Education Progressive Education Network (PEN), a student organization aimed at forming meaningful networks of innovators who propel education forward. Through PEN, she launched Ed Harmony the first annual education innovation and networking showcase at the Harvard Innovation Lab. She is currently developing a 21st century skill curriculum and is passionate about education that empowers others to think critically and meaningfully about their role in the world around them. Ms. Lee's other passions include eating exotic foods, learning about different cultures, and discovering the good in people.

Randy Tarnowski, *Ed.M., Harvard Graduate School of Education*
Randy Tarnowski is a current Masters degree candidate at the Harvard Graduate School of Education. Previously, as Executive Assistant at the Korean-American Educational Commission, Mr. Tarnowski managed the Fulbright Senior Scholar and Junior Researcher programs in order to foster cross-national partnerships. As Program Manager for WorldTeach, Mr. Tarnowski supports international teaching programs in over thirteen countries. He is a previous recipient of the Fulbright grant to South Korea, as well as the Young Kil & Sunny Kim Scholarship from the Korean American Scholarship

Foundation. In terms of research, Mr. Tarnowski is interested in the "internationalization" movement within higher education institutions and its implications on global equity. Mr. Tarnowski's written work can be found in a Hard Questions on Global Educational Change (Teachers College Press, 2016) and in The Routledge Handbook for Global Child Welfare (Routledge, 2016).

| Appendix III |

List of Contributors

● ● ●

Introduction

Hungsoo S. Kim, *Korean*
President, Center for Asia Leadership Initiatives
MPA, Harvard Kennedy School of Government

Asia Leadership Youth Camp

Janice Tan Sue Wei, *Malaysian*
Year 11, Sri KDU International School, Malaysia

Michelle S Lee, *Malaysian*
Undergraduate Degree Candidate, Minerva Schools at KGI, US

Bryan Chay, *Singaporean*
Year 11, Alice Smith School, Malaysia

Jonson Tham, *Malaysian*
Grade 10, Sunway International School, Malaysia

Ben Ang Zi Qi, *Malaysian*
A–Levels, Sunway College, Malaysia

Kamaleshwaran Ganeson, *Malaysian*
BSc (Hons) in Psychology Candidate, Sunway University, Malaysia

Ong Qian Chern, *Malaysian*
BSc (Hons) in Information Technology (Computer Networking and Security) Candidate, Sunway University, Malaysia

Loh Lynn Way, *Malaysian*
Canadian International Matriculation Program (CIMP), Sunway College, Malaysia

Global Leadership Trek

Mengheng Lim, *Cambodian*
Structural Engineer at GBC Engineers (BSc in Civil Engineering from Zaman University, Cambodia)

Maika Tsuchiya, *Japanese*
Grade 12, Narita High School, Japan

Amirhossein Rahbari, *Iranian*
A–Levels, Sunway College, Malaysia

Central Asia Youth Leadership Camp

Aleksandra Kan, *Uzbekistan*
BSc in Petroleum Engineering Candidate, Gubkin Russian State University of Oil and Gas, Uzbekistan

Anastasiia Iun, *Kyrgyzstan*
MA in Psychological Counseling Candidate, American University of Central Asia, Kyrgyzstan

Anjela Kamalova, *Uzbekistan*
4th Year, Japanese Language and Culture, Tashkent State Institute of Oriental Studies, Uzbekistan

Evgeniy Kim, *Uzbekistan*
BA (Hons) in Business Administration Candidate, Westminster International University, Uzbekistan

Zarina Shemdanova, *Uzbekistan*
Korean Language and Literature, Tashkent State Pedagogical University Named After Nizami, Uzbekistan

Trilateral Leadership Summit III

Megumi Konishi, *Japanese*
Junior, Shibuya Senior High School, Japan

Annie Dawon Lee, *Korean*
Senior, Phillips Academy, United States

Shiina Yuri, *Japanese*
Senior, Rakunan High School, Japan

Jiho Hwang, *Korean*
Sophomore, Jeonju University High School, Korea

Alex Wookyung Lee, *Korean*
Senior, Wonkwang Girls' High School, Korea

Hinako Telengut, *Japanese*
Junior, Ritsumeikan Keisho High School, Japan